Reforming the Malawian Public Sector

Retrospectives and Prospectives

Edited by
Richard Tambulasi

CODESRIA

Council for the Development of Social Science Research in Africa

ISBN: 978-2-86978-314 -0

Typesetting: Daouda Thiam
Cover Design: Ibrahima Fofana
Printing: Imprimerie Saint-Paul, Dakar, Senegal

Distributed in Africa by CODESRIA
Distributed elsewhere by African Books Collective, Oxford, UK
Website: www.africanbookscollective.com

The Council for the Development of Social Science Research in Africa (CODESRIA) is an independent organisation whose principal objectives are to facilitate research, promote research-based publishing and create multiple forums geared towards the exchange of views and information among African researchers. All these are aimed at reducing the fragmentation of research in the continent through the creation of thematic research networks that cut across linguistic and regional boundaries.

CODESRIA publishes a quarterly journal, *Africa Development*, the longest standing Africa-based social science journal; *Afrika Zamani*, a journal of history; the *African Sociological Review*; the *African Journal of International Affairs*; *Africa Review of Books* and the *Journal of Higher Education in Africa*. The Council also co-publishes the *Africa Media Review*; *Identity, Culture and Politics: An Afro-Asian Dialogue*; *The African Anthropologist* and the *Afro-Arab Selections for Social Sciences*. The results of its research and other activities are also disseminated through its Working Paper Series, Green Book Series, Monograph Series, Book Series, Policy Briefs and the CODESRIA Bulletin. Select CODESRIA publications are also accessible online at www.codesria.org.

CODESRIA would like to express its gratitude to the Swedish International Development Cooperation Agency (SIDA/SAREC), the International Development Research Centre (IDRC), the Ford Foundation, the MacArthur Foundation, the Carnegie Corporation, the Norwegian Agency for Development Cooperation (NORAD), the Danish Agency for International Development (DANIDA), the French Ministry of Cooperation, the United Nations Development Programme (UNDP), the Netherlands Ministry of Foreign Affairs, the Rockefeller Foundation, FINIDA, the Canadian International Development Agency (CIDA), IIEP/ADEA, OECD, IFS, OXFAM America, UN/UNICEF, the African Capacity Building Foundation (ACBF) and the Government of Senegal for supporting its research, training and publication programmes.

Contents

Notes on Authors v

Critical Perspectives on Public Sector Reforms: An Introduction
    Richard I.C. Tambulasi 1

Public-sector Reforms and Decentralisation of Public Services: Lessons
From Malawi (1994-2006)
    Asiyati Lorraine Chiweza 29

Public-private Partnership in the Malawian Local Assemblies: A Failed
Reform Package?
    Happy M. Kayuni 57

No Key Opens Every Door: The Failure of NPM-Based Performance
Contracting in Malawi
    Richard I.C. Tambulasi 69

Resurrecting the Developmental State in Malawi: Reflections and Lessons
from the 2005/2006 Fertiliser Subsidy Programme
Setting the Context
    Blessings Chinsinga 81

Notes on Authors

Richard I.C. Tambulasi is a Senior Lecturer in the Department of Political and Administrative Studies, Chancellor College, University of Malawi. He is currently reading for his PhD in Public Policy and Management at the University of Manchester in England. He holds a Bachelor and a Master of Public Administration from the University of Stellenbosch in South Africa, and a Bachelor of Arts in Public Administration from the University of Malawi. His areas of interest include public policy, public management, public governance and political science. He has published over 16 articles in international journals. He has also contributed chapters to some books in his field. One of his journal articles entitled "Who is Fooling Who?: New Public Management–Oriented Management Accounting and Political Control in the Malawi's Local Governance" which appeared in the 2007 *Journal of Accounting and Organizational Change,* won the 2008 Highly Recommended Paper Emerald Awards for Excellence.

Asiyati Chiweza is a Senior Lecturer and head of the Department of Political and Administrative Studies, Chancellor College, University of Malawi. She holds a Doctor of Philosophy in Social Sciences (Public Policy) from Curtin University, Australia; a Master of Public Administration from Dalhousie University, Canada; and a Bachelor of Social Science from University of Malawi. Her fields of research and expertise include decentralisation and local governance, public policy, development administration and public financial management. She has done extensive research in the field of decentralisation and local government and has published book chapters and journal articles in local and international journals.

Happy M. Kayuni is a Senior Lecturer and deputy head of the Department of Political and Administrative Studies, University of Malawi. He holds a Bachelor of Arts in Public Administration from the University of Malawi as well as a Bachelor and a Master of Public Administration from the University of Stellenbosch in South Africa. His areas of specialisation include party politics, management and public governance and development. He has published more than seven peer-reviewed journal articles and book chapters in these areas. He has been teaching, among other courses, Strategic Management, International Relations and Development Studies.

Blessings Chinsinga holds an MPhil and a PhD in Development Studies from the University of Cambridge, UK and the University of Mainz, Germany. He is currently based at the Department of Political and Administrative Studies, Chancellor College, University of Malawi as an Associate Professor, specialising in institutions and development, public policy analysis, development administration, rural livelihood and local level politics. He has published over 20 journal articles and book chapters, and a book based on his PhD dissertation titled *Decentralization, Democracy and Poverty Reduction in Malawi* (2007).

1

Critical Perspectives on Public Sector Reforms: An Introduction

Richard I.C. Tambulasi

This publication is a memorial to the late Professor Guy Mhone, whose rare academic stamina and rigour shaped the research subfield of public sector reforms and developmentalism in Africa. We argue in this publication that the neo-liberal new public management-based public sector reforms that Malawi, like most African countries, adopted under the influence of donor institutions have not led to the promised efficiency and effectiveness in the running of the public sector. At best, these reforms have been poorly implemented, as the necessary institutional infrastructure for their effective implementation has been absent. As a result, some of these reforms have either been abandoned (for example, performance contracting, as discussed in chapter four) or face massive challenges in implementation with little prospect of achieving their goals (for example decentralisation and public-private-partnerships, as discussed in chapters two and three).

The underlying problems are that donors have dominated the reform processes and, under their influence, the state has withdrawn from its developmental mission. The reforms themselves have further eroded the capacity of the state to participate in viable developmental projects. The situation reaffirms the prediction by Polidano (1998:285) that 'public sector reforms in developing countries will resemble a landscape dotted with ruined edifices and abandoned skeletal structures'. Nevertheless, this publication sees some rays of hope in the return of the developmental state in Malawi (see chapter five). Malawi's overwhelming success in its 2005/6 fertiliser subsidy programme, which the government embarked on singlehandedly despite donors' unwillingness to support, demonstrates the developmental potential the state has so that, if replicated in other sectors of the economy, can lead to higher levels of development.

Contextual Background

Malawi, like many African countries, has been subjected to a plethora of public sector reforms. In fact, Africa contains perhaps the most over-reformed states in the world, despite their mostly recent origins. External actors have dominated the African reform platform, and the reform podium has been characterised by coercive policy reform transfers rather than country-initiated rational learning (Dolowitz and Marsh 2000; Common 2001; Evans 2004). For instance, Therkildesen (2001:3) observes that the reforms initiated by the World Bank and the International Monetary Fund in Africa in the 1980s were twice as many as those in the rest of the developing world. Since then, donor involvement has only increased.

These externally imposed public sector reforms can be traced to the period after decolonisation, when the departing colonial masters left their institutional infrastructures for the operation of the former colonies. Malawi and other former British colonies inherited the Westminster–Whitehall model based on the 'parliamentary system, electoral competition, a neutral civil service, decentralisation, the rule of the Western-style law and the protection of civil and political rights' (Minogue 2002:122). However, most of these reforms were adopted mainly as a way of facilitating the independence negotiations. What was in the minds of many African leaders at the time was the question of how the post-colonial state could be instrumental in social and economic development. The argument was that the colonial state had merely been an exploitative instrument for the achievement of colonial interests rather than national development. In the colonial state, any development projects that were embarked on were mainly intended to facilitate colonial reign rather than holistic national development.

The key post-independence goal, therefore, was to develop and deploy the state machinery for higher levels of development. This goal was supported by the 'emergence of the activist and interventionist model of the state, based on the assumed superiority of the bureaucratic model of large-scale organisations' (Minogue 2002:133). This, in turn, led to the formation of 'new but poor states committed to economic betterment: the developmental state' (Minogue 2002:133). In the case of Malawi, Mhone (1992:11) tells us that the 'economic landscape has been drastically and, in many ways, irreversibly transformed by the purposeful intervention of the state', while Minogue (2002:133) notes that the central assumption behind the activist state model 'was that a crucial role of the state was to make good the deficiencies of the private market'. Some states, such as Botswana, were successful with this model, owing to their visionary and developmentally-minded leadership. In other cases, the state became predatory and riddled with corruption, as happened in Zaire (Mkandawire 2001; Evans 1989), or dictatorial and totalitarian, as in Malawi (Mhone 1992). As Mhone illustrates, the Malawi case consisted of 'mutually determining and reinforcing political apparatuses of authoritarianism, paternalism and repression, and economic relations of dominion and exploitation' (Mhone 1992:1). Such negative examples, together with the general failure of government interventions elsewhere, made donor institutions rethink the role of the state in development and emphasise the use of the market.

The dismantling of the developmental state in Africa began when the ideological support basis for state intervention was swept away with the end of the Cold War, and "free market' capitalism, multiparty democratic and 'good governance' came to be seen as universal virtues. As a result, developing countries were required by the World Bank and the IMF to adopt neo-liberal structural adjustment programmes (SAPs). In the realm of public administration, governments worldwide began replacing their bureaucratic and state-driven public services with the market-oriented new public management (NPM) model. The NPM has its basis in the neo-liberal economic theory that 'combined an attack on the inefficiency of public bureaucracies with strictness on the flawed nature of the activist state' (Minogue 2002:134). Alongside SAPs, donor institutions begun to push for the implementation of NPM reforms within wider good governance programmes as conditions for aid in developing countries. NPM required a major transformation of the public sector in developing countries.

The New Public Management

Public sector reforms are commonplace. They are 'planned systematic changes to the structure, processes and operation of the public sector' (Tambulasi and Kayuni 2007a:335) which are 'sanctioned as the means to bring about the desired changes' (Turner and Hulme 1997:106). The NPM paradigm has been the main public sector reform model in many countries for the past decade. NPM is now so popular that if one mentions the 'words public sector reform... many listeners will take it for granted that you are talking about the new public management' (Polidano 1998:773). With the introduction of the new public management, traditional public administration which is synonymous with bureaucracy, is 'slowly trekking to the grave' (Tambulasi 2007:303). In fact, NPM aims to change and replace traditional public administration entirely (Batley and Larbi 2004; Pollitt and Bouckaert 2000; Hughes 1998; Tambulasi 2007).

Many authors have come up with different conceptions of NPM, but as an 'evolutionally and continuously developing concept' (Hoque 2005:4), NPM's constitutive components are highly debatable. What is central to all NPM arguments is the implementation of market-based principles in the running of the public sector. According to Lane (1997:5), NPM entails 'competitive government, injecting competition into service delivery; enterprising government, earning rather than spending; and market oriented government, leveraging change through the market'. The rationale is that the private sector is efficient due to effective management practices. Therefore, in order to make the public sector equally efficient, the same market principles have to be applied. The argument is that 'organizations need to be efficient, effective and to provide value for money' (Turner and Hulme 1997:106). A comprehensive attempt to define the basic components of NPM can be found in Christopher Hood (1991). Hood's account of NPM's 'doctrinal' components can be summarised as 'disaggregation + competition + incentivisation' (Dunleavy and Margetts 2000:13). The case studies presented in this book are organised around these themes. In essence, disaggregation is mostly represented by decentralization, competition is exemplified by public-private partnerships, and incentivisation is akin to performance contracting.

Disaggregation and Decentralisation

Decentralisation is 'one of the principal themes of NPM' (Mimba, Helden and Tillema 2007:198) as NPM champions a shift to 'disaggregation of units in the public sector' (Hood 1991:5). This means the devolution of management control with improved reporting and monitoring mechanisms (Hope and Chikulo 2000:27). It emphasises the breaking up of 'monolithic' (Hood 1991) public sector machinery into small manageable units. This entails decentralisation. In this case 'decentralisation is generally prescribed as a means of liberating potential shackles by bureaucratic restrictions' (Metcalfe and Richards 1990:77). Decentralisation is generally understood as the 'transfer of power from the centre to the periphery' (Tambulasi and Kayuni 2007b:164). Similarly, Steunenburg and Mol (1997:234) capture decentralisation as 'public sector reform conceived as changes in the distribution of tasks between different levels of government'. A more encompassing definition is provided by Rondinelli (2006:433), who looks at decentralisation as the 'transfer of responsibilities and authority to lower levels within the central government (deconcentration), or from the centre to local government units (devolution) and nongovernmental organisations (delegation), or from government to the private sector (deregulation and privatisation)'. The value of Rondinelli's definition is that it spells out the variations of decentralisation – deconcentration, devolution, delegation, deregulation and privatisation. These variations are further explored by Chiweza in the second chapter of this book.

Bangura and Larbi (2006:8) observe that 'among NPM reforms, decentralised management has been one of the key trends in developing countries and has taken different forms'. These forms include administrative, institutional, political and fiscal dimensions. Administratively, decentralisation has meant the transfer of managerial authority and responsibility vertically from higher levels to lower levels of management (Tambulasi and Kayuni 2007b). Institutional decentralisation is a variant of administrative decentralisation. It refers to the 'administrative bodies, systems and mechanisms, both local and intergovernmental, which help to manage and support decentralisation' (Smoke 2003:10). At the political level, decentralisation is regarded as the 'creation of bodies separated by law from the nation centre in which local (elected) representatives are given formal power to decide on a range of public matters' (Mawhood 1993:2). Local elections and greater civic participation are the hallmarks of political decentralisation. It is for this reason that this variant of decentralisation has usually been linked to democracy and good governance, formulating what is commonly referred to as 'democratic decentralisation'. Fiscal decentralisation is the engine that drives the whole decentralisation process; without well defined fiscal decentralisation, the other dimensions of decentralisation would have little impact (Smoke 2003:10). Fiscal decentralisation can either be political or administrative or both, but its distinctive feature is that it has a financial responsibility and authority component (Tambulasi and Kayuni 2007b). Smoke (2003), however, advises the adoption of a broader economic view that goes beyond finance. In this view, fiscal decentralisation should be understood as the 'assignment of responsibilities, including sectoral functions, as well as the assignment of own-source revenues to sub-national governments' (Smoke 2003:10).

Decentralisation reforms have been widespread in developing countries. Mimba, Helden and Tillema (2007:198) claim that '63 of the 75 developing countries with a population of more than five million are actively employing decentralisation'. The goal of decentralisation is to increase effectiveness and efficiency in service delivery, as local authorities are 'closer to the people and therefore likely to respond better to their preferences' (Bangura and Larbi 2006:16). In this regard, decentralisation has been a 'major reform strategy for handling complexity in the public sector' (Lane 1997:9). In addition, decentralisation is seen as a mechanism for reducing the costs of bureaucratic control, and thereby increasing the effectiveness of central government policy-making (Steunenburg and Mol 1997:234). Mimba, Helden and Tillema (2007:198) observe that, in some cases, decentralisation has been championed to increase participation in government and improve the mobilisation and use of resources. Within the context of NPM, decentralisation is seen as the means of separating the 'core policy-making and regulatory functions of ministries from those dealing with implementation (Bangura and Larbi 2006:8). The expected results are that:

- governments are able to provide high-quality services that citizens value;

- there is increased managerial autonomy, particularly by reducing central administrative controls;

- there is a mechanism for demanding, measuring and rewarding both organisational and individual performance;

- managers acquire human and technological resources to meet performance targets;

- there is receptiveness to competition and open-mindedness about which public purposes should be performed by public servants as opposed to the private sector;
- there is improved economic and managerial efficiency or effectiveness;
- there is better governance (Hope and Chikulo 2000:29).

The actual results of decentralised systems in Africa are a mixed bag. While there are a few patches of success, decentralisation in most African countries has either failed (Olowu 1990), led to unintended consequences (Tambulasi and Kayuni 2007b) or is struggling with a plethora of challenges (Chiweza in this book). These are the issues that Chiweza discusses in the next chapter of this book. She argues that the critical premise of local government has not significantly changed and that institutions are still fragile, making local government appear to be an extension of the central government. As Hussein (2003:271) observes, the failure of decentralisation in Malawi has been a result of 'little clarity on how community-based institutions are integrated into the local government system' and inadequate institutional, political, socio-economic and administrative frameworks to support the decentralisation drive. Additionally, in Malawi, as in many African countries, there are 'widespread self-seeking tendencies' (Chinsinga 2005:529) in the decentralised system, which have led the whole decentralisation process to 'open a new window for corruption' (Tambulasi and Kayuni 2007b:168). This leads us to the doubts that Dauda (2006:291) has about the 'viability' of decentralisation as a vehicle for development in sub-Saharan Africa. In this regard, Africa in general and Malawi in particular have not attained the decentralisation dream they intended to achieve when they 'passed new constitutions and laws' (Smoke 2003:12).

Competition and Public-private Partnerships

NPM champions the adoption of private-sector styles of management in the public sector with the aim of attaining effectiveness, efficiency and improved service delivery. To achieve these goals, NPM demands a 'shift to greater competition in the public sector' (Hood 1991:5), since 'rivalry between diverse producers can be used to lower costs and improve standards' (Olowu 1990:4). Competition is thus one of the dominant themes in NPM literature. Instruments for attaining greater competition include privatisation, commercialisation and market testing (Olowu 1990:4) along with the use of public-private partnerships (PPPs). In general, PPPs are 'increasingly heralded as an innovative policy tool for remedying the lack of dynamism in traditional public service delivery' (Jamali 2004:103). In particular, Tambulasi (2007:205) emphasises that NPM 'considers the use of public-private partnerships as one of the tools for management to achieve effective outcomes'. PPPs are seen as a means of obtaining 'greater discipline and parsimony in resource use' with the aim of 'doing more with fewer resources' (Hood 1991:5). It is against this backdrop that the key phrases in this realm include 'value for money' and 'better services at less cost' (Lane 1997:10). At the centre of PPPs are the use of shared authority and responsibility, shared liabilities and risks, joint investment and shared reward/mutual benefit (Tambulasi 2007:305). According to Grouts (1997:54), the central feature of PPP projects is as follows:

> [T]he private sector funds and builds the asset, and it is the flow of services from the asset that is sold to the public sector; that is, the obligation on the part of the government is to purchase, directly or indirectly, a flow of services over time rather than the capital asset that provides the services.

The aim is to 'drive a wedge between public services and their delivery, creating a category of services that are still public services but which are privately delivered' (Ontario Federation of Labour 2005:2). In this case, PPPs 'expand public services and reduce the size of the public sector at the same time' (Ontario Federation of Labour 2005:1). PPPs have had massive publicity due to the negative experiences with privatisation in many developing countries. In this regard, PPPs have been regarded as a means of introducing supervised services from the private sector into the public realm. Lane (1997:10) emphasises this point by adding that PPPs are an 'insertion of [market-based] decision mechanisms into the public sector without resorting to privatisation'. They are a form of 'structured cooperation between public and private parties in the planning, construction and/or exploitation of infrastructural facilities in which they share or reallocate risks, costs, benefits, resources and responsibilities' (Koppenjan 2005:137). It must be noted, however, that the PPP process is not simply a charitable involvement of the private sector under the philanthropic themes of social responsibility. It is about securing better value for money in the delivery of clearly specified outputs (Tambulasi 2007:313-314). Thus any 'subsidy relationships where government does not share the risk in a private project' (Koppenjan 2005:137) does not constitute a PPP.

While the literature of PPPs is full of invigorating language and promises of efficiency, the reality in many developing countries has been very disappointing. The implementation of PPPs in African countries, including Malawi, has encountered many serious challenges to the achievement of competition and efficiency goals. These challenges are thoroughly discussed by Happy Kayuni in relation to PPPs at the Malawian local government level in the third chapter of this book. Kayuni argues that the Malawi local assemblies are not fully prepared to efficiently and effectively embark on PPPs, as they do not posses key success factors and attributes. To be effective, PPPs require specific conducive environments that most African states do not possess, such as favourable investment environments, strong private consortiums, appropriate risk allocation, available financial markets, economic viability, effective procurement, project implementability, reliable contractual arrangements, government guarantee and favourable overall economic conditions (Li et al. 2005; Jamali 2004; Zhang 2005). In addition, PPPs may simply not be viable in developing countries, where there tend to be high cost restraints on innovation and differing or conflicting objectives among stakeholders, not to mention the high tendering costs and time-consuming, complex negotiations required in establishing PPPs (Li et al. 2005:459).

Apart from these critical factors, the implementation of PPPs in Africa has also been problematic due the flaws inherent in PPPs themselves, which make PPPs 'not suitable for all policy areas' (Flinders 2005:225). In the first place, PPPs are very risky, and, as Shaoul argues, 'far from transferring risk to the private sector, PPP transfers the risk to the government, workforce and the public as users and taxpayers' (cited in Flinders 2005:226). The claims of cost reduction and greater efficiency are also questionable. Transaction costs tend to increase in a PPP arrangement because of the multiplicity of actors and the hybridism of the organisational forms, with 'secondary quasi-autonomous organisations [that are] created to oversee and regulate the activities of these PPP' (Flinders 2005:227). Moreover, conflicts of interests are also common in PPPs (Jamali 2004:108). The private-sector actors are, in most instances, profit-driven, while the public-sector actors are motivated by social considerations. This picture is further complicated when the public actors engage in self-seeking activities and corrupt deals with the private actors. Koppenjan (2005:136) observes that these conflicting interests lead to a 'hesitancy on the part of those engaged in public-private interactions, leading to unilateral public planning followed by difficult contract negotiations'. As a result, PPPs 'may in practice involve little close cooperation' (Jamali 2004:108). According to Flinders (2005:228), PPPs 'disrupt traditional accountability structures' and open avenues to corruption. Thus, the real risks associated with PPPs are not commercial but governance-related, involing neglect of 'traditional checks and balances afforded to major projects' (Hodge 2004:47). Moreover, PPPs 'achieve cost reduction at the expense of democracy and equity' (Jamali 2004:108).

Incentivisation and Performance Contracting

Incentivisation is another dominant practice preached by the NPM movement. The aim is to bring incentives to public sector managers so that they carry out market-based private sector practices and remain competitive. At the hub of incentivisation is the practice of performance contracting. Performance contracting requires managerial positions to be 'contractualised' (Oluwo 2002:3); public managers work according to performance contracts that stipulate specific targets, and managerial performance is measured according to the extent these targets are attained (Tambulasi 2007:303). The principle here is the establishment of a reciprocal relationship in which managers 'undertake to meet explicit targets or carry out specific activities. In return, government commits itself to provide various resource inputs and to give managers more authority over operations, including budgeting, purchasing and personnel' (Therkildsen 2001:27). In this regard, 'failure to fulfil the performance contract would then entail that the employment contract has been invalidated' (Lane 1999:184). To be feasible, performance contracts require the establishment of 'explicit standards of measures of performance' with a clear 'definition of goals, targets, indicators of success, preferably expressed in quantitative terms, especially for professional services' (Hood 1991:4). Consequently, performance contracting calls for 'hands on professional management in the public sector ... [and] active, visible, discretionary control of organisations from named persons at the top [who are] free to manage' (Hood 1991:5). The catch phrase here is 'let managers manage' (Olowu 1990:3). According to Tambulasi (2007:302), this arrangement ensures that managers effectively and efficiently deliver the goods and services the public expects them to deliver. In addition, it enhances accountability and efficiency mechanisms because accountability requires 'clear assignment of responsibility for action' and 'statement of goals', while efficiency 'requires a hard look at objectives' (Hood 1991:4).

In general, African countries have experimented with performance contracting with much difficulty. The practice has encountered challenges that have led either to undesirable consequences or the practice being abandoned altogether. In in the case of Malawi, Tambulasi argues (chapter four) that performance contracting failed and was consequently abandoned because, like other NPM tools, its successful implementation depends on favourable country-specific institutional contexts and conducive environments which Malawi, like many developing countries, does not possess. This is in line with Larbi's observation (2006:39) that the implementation of performance contracting has 'been problematic, mainly because a number of critical institutional preconditions are often absent to make the system work as expected'. This is true even for some developed countries. In a Norwegian study, for instance, Christensen and Laegreid (2001:79) found that performance contracts have 'cultural problems with getting adapted in Norway'. For developing countries, the situation is even worse. As Therkildsen (2001:32) notes, the application of performance management in South Africa, Uganda and Zimbabwe 'appears to be unrealistic'. Experience in these countries has shown that performance contracts 'rarely improve incentives and may do more harm than good' to already poor incentive structures (Therkildsen 2000:31). In addition, Mimba, Helden and Tillema (2007:199) observe that performance management in many African countries has increased corruption; the system's 'high informality ... gives managers much more discretion to hire employees and spend money as they wish, which provides them with more opportunities for corruption'. Moreover, there are also performance measurement problems that exacerbate the situation. Performance measurement is 'complex and controversial', as measurement standards are often based on 'assumptions not generally met under prevailing conditions' (Therkildsen 2001:31). In most cases, there is an 'absence of a common and broadly accepted framework for defining what good performance means' (Therkildsen 2001:31).

Accounting for the Dismal Performance of the Reforms

The forgoing discussion along with the next three papers presented in this volume highlight the fact that NPM has not found a comfortable home in developing countries. As the specific studies on Malawi will show, the challenges have been massive and, in some cases, the reforms have been abandoned altogether. The critical aspects of the NPM reforms that have made their implementation problematic include the influential role of donors, the appropriateness of the NPM reforms and the divorcing the state from development. The following sections of this paper discuss each of these aspects in turn.

The Role of Donors

The study of public sector reforms in any African country would be incomplete if the role of donor countries, institutions and agencies were not highlighted. This is because, behind almost each and every reform effort in African countries, there have been donors acting either explicitly or implicitly. As Batley (1999) observes, 'there are cases where reforms have been advanced in the absence of real local support, but none where international agencies have been absent' (cited in Therkildesen 2001:3). Similarly, Polidano (2001) points out that the 'power of the purse, plus some quite definite ideas regarding what sort of reforms are desirable, has led donor agencies to take centre stage in the design of reform initiatives'. The NPM reforms are no exception. The NPM tools have 'tended to be applied through powerful international donor agencies and financial institutions' (Larbi 2006:31), to such an extent that some scholars see the NPM reforms in developing countries as 'donor conditionality' and 'imposition' (Mxakato-Diseko 2008:1; Common 1998:442) leading to the 'export of managerial reforms in low income countries' (Bangura and Larbi 2006:20). Moreover in most African countries 'donors are *de facto* an integrated part of both the policy making and the budgetary processes' (Therkildesen 2001:8).

To make matters worse, donors have transferred the NPM reforms wholesale in a one-size-fits-all fashion without considering the specific social, political, economic and institutional environments within which the reforms are to be implemented. The reasoning has been that reforms that have worked well elsewhere will work well everywhere. However, as Tambulasi (chapter four) argues, in public sector reforms there is no such a thing as a magic key that opens every door. Specific reforms are applicable for specific problems in particular countries' environmental contexts. In addition, donors mostly carry on with reform initiatives even when there are clear indications that the country concerned does not want them. For instance, Hirschmann (1993:126) observes that, in Malawi, 'donors are mostly set on continuing with their programmes whether or not the Malawians show evidence of, or even concern for, maintaining them'.

Moreover, there is huge competition among donors for aid markets. This competition sees a multiplicity of donors in a country all financing the same projects, thus creating coordination problems. For instance, in Malawi, as of June 1996, seven donor institutions – IMF, UNDP, UK/ODA, USAID, European Union, CIDA, and the World Bank – were providing assistance in the area of civil service reform alone (Ademolekun, Kulemeka and Laleye 1997:218). Such competition leads to both 'reform overload' (Therkildesen 2001:8) and 'capacity overload' (Ademolekun, Kulemeka and Laleye 1997:218) and 'further slows down the implementation of development projects and programmes' (Ademolekun, Kulemeka and Laleye 1997:218).

The recipient African countries have little choice but to take up the reforms pushed by donors, even though they may be well aware of their inappropriateness and likely undesirable consequences. The cost of refusing donor-driven reforms is much-needed foreign aid and loans that most developing countries cannot afford to lose. As a result, there has been an enculturation of what we might call the 'do-not-refuse-donor-money syndrome' in the entire civil service. NPM reforms have thus been taken up 'without any questions being asked regarding their suitability for meeting the needs of the continent in a sustained manner' (Mxakato-Diseko 2008:1). For instance, in a study on Malawi, Hirschmann (1993:126) observed that the 'culture of the civil service requires that nobody be seen as a person who is blocking aid', making local officials unable to 'question seriously the continued flow of resources, opportunities and their accompanying evaluations and recommendations'. Against the backdrop of this baleful donor influence, the poor performance of reforms in developing countries is hardly surprising.

Appropriateness of the Reforms

Donor institutions and all the other bearers of the NPM gospel have preached it as a magic bullet that can rectify all public-sector problems regardless of country-specific conditions. NPM is regarded as 'public management for all seasons' (Hood 1991) and as an 'example of globalization at work' (United Nations 2001). However, as Asiyati Chiweza, Happy Kayuni and Richard Tambulasi illustrate in this volume, the NPM is 'not a panacea for all the problems in the public sector' (Larbi 2006:47). The reality is that, in most cases, 'public sector reform realities may be quite a different matter, as there tends to be a huge distance between lofty theory and down-to-earth practice' (Lane 1997:1). For most developing countries, NPM instruments are simply not appropriate for the prevailing social, cultural, political, administrative, institutional and economic environments. It is in this vein that Minogue (2002:134) alludes to the 'difficulty of making such policy transfers across different political and bureaucratic cultures'. As a result, in most developing countries, the 'conditions on which new management practices are premised may not be present' (Bangura and Larbi 2006:11), resulting in numerous suitability and sustainability hiccups. The effects of context in the applicability of NPM are well illustrated by Larbi (2006:26):

> Context does matter in the application of the NPM reforms. Specific NPM approaches may work better in some contexts than others. It is important to bear these differences in mind because they increase or decrease the chances of NPM being a good fit in developing countries. Countries also differ in their capacities to adopt particular NPM techniques

Apart from context of application, there are issues about the contents of NPM attributes themselves. In this regard, the NPM instruments have been seen to be problematic in effectively delivering on efficiency promises. In most cases, the private sector principles of NPM have not been compatible with public-sector values. As a result, these NPM principles have failed to perform as a magic medicine to cure the public-sector ills and deficiencies. As Larbi (1999:33) observes, the 'assumption that involving the private sector makes for higher levels of performance is given only a partial support by evidence'. In most cases, it is 'doubtful whether these private sector management concepts can easily be transposed into, let alone simply imitated by, the public sector' (Kickert 1997:183). Moreover, there are now many new sets of challenges due to issues related to contemporary market-driven public sector reforms (Haque 2001:71). Thus, although the performance of 'our public service pre-NPM left a lot to be desired, an examination of the solution offered by the NPM reveals tendencies that may have deleterious effects on building a coherent professionalism' (Mxakato-Diseko 2008:12). For instance, research has unveiled unintended consequences that arise in the areas of accountability (Haque 2001:71; Lane 1997:12), democratic ideals (Tambulasi 2007), national unity and equality (Larbi 2006:45). These findings lend weight to Halligan's (1997:39) observation that the NPM 'framework was a precondition for long-term reform but was insufficient as a comprehensive solution to complex pressures of the public sector'.

Divorcing the State from Development

The dismal performance of NPM tools can also be explained as a result of divorcing the state from developmental interventions and by letting private-sector governance tools dictate events through quasi-markets. NPM reforms are designed to reduce the role of the public sector to that of 'steering rather than rowing' (Osborne and Gaebler 1992), making it 'hands-tied' (Mhone 2003:4) so that it only plays the role of 'night watchman' (Mkandawire 2001:292). Haque (2001:70) attests that, in the United States, the 'whole idea of reinventing government was to assign public services with a catalyzing or facilitating role, to reinforce the leading role of the private sector, and to ask the public sector to 'steer' rather than 'row'. The same principles have been applied to developing countries. As Mxakato-Diseko (2008:1) observes, through NPM reforms, the 'World Bank and the IMF sought to solve what they perceived as the problem of too much state as a key factor iinhibiting development'.

The irony, however, is that the state is required to facilitate its own replacement by the private sector by providing conducive environments for the NPM reforms. Not surprisingly, there have been complaints about lack of ownership and commitment of the local political leaders. For example, in the case of Malawi, Ademolekun, Kulemeka and Laleye (1997:220) observe that there was 'no champion for reform at the political level result[ing] into a rather unfocused and uncoordinated approach to both the formulation and implementation or reform measures'. However, by underplaying the role of the state, the NPM reforms 'entirely miss the point that such virtues can only be instituted and sustained by politics' (Leftwich 1995:421). In addition, the state machinery has been blamed for not having the capacity to implement NPM reforms when the reforms entail more emphasis on market capacities rather than bureaucratic ones; yet, paradoxically, the essential capacity of the state critical to the implementation of the reforms is being eroded by the same reforms (Mkandawire 2001). According to Haque (2001:70), the capacity of the public sector 'has been diminished due to the restructuring of its financial and human resources under the recent market driven reforms'.

Capacity problems with NPM also arise when the state in developing countries is dismantled too soon, before it effectively builds the prerequisite administrative stamina that lays a solid foundation for market interventions. As a result, NPM has been created on an 'empty managerial shell' (Bangura and Larbi 2006:21). It is against this backdrop that there is a dire need for 'ascertaining the publicness' (Haque 2001:69) of the public sector. As Mhone argues, a mode of administration needs to be adopted 'that allows for highly coordinated' [interventions] … along developmentalist lines', as the 'present forms are such that one hand does not know what the other is doing' (Mhone 2003:18). This reformulation is very important because, as we have highlighted in terms of NPM, reforms that 'ignore the core developmental missions of states may not only yield poor results but also undermine political settlements and make it difficult to reconstruct failing states, institutions and economies' (Bangura and Larbi 2006:3). This brings us to the u-turn that Blessings Chinsinga proposes in chapter five of this volume. His proposal is for the resurrection of the developmental state, an option we discuss in more detail below.

Re-enter the Developmental State

The casualties of neo-liberal reforms in state governance highlighted above have prompted many stakeholders, both at the international and national level, to consider the reintroduction of the state into the mainstream running of public affairs. Due to the unpleasant consequences of divorcing the state from development, the developmental state option is once again being proposed as a viable trajectory for socio-economic development and poverty reduction in developing countries. As Leftwich (1995:422) argues, NPM tools amount to 'narrow administrative models of development [that] simply evacuate politics from developmental processes'. It is therefore time, Leftwich argues 'to bring politics firmly back in to the analysis and promotion of development' (1995:422). Fritz and Menocal (2007:53) note that the 'developmental state is back at the centre of the international policy debate', with Clare Short, the former United Kingdom Secretary of State for International Development, declaring that the importance of 'strong and effective states' has been recognised and that the 'era of complete enmity to the public sector in general and to state provision in particular is coming to an end' (Short, cited in Larbi 2006:47). This is the argument that Blessings Chinsinga advances in the final chapter of this book. Based on the successful state-funded fertilizer subsidy programme in Malawi in 2005/2006 – which donors were unwilling to support – Chinsinga argues that Malawi acted developmentally and provided a model for state leadership this could be used as the basis for a viable framework for a successful developmental state in Malawi.

Debates on the developmental state have attracted much scholarly attention over the years, with overwhelming agreement that the 'Asian Tigers', along with some of the immediate post-colonial African regimes (Mkandawire 2001; Mhone 2003), can be regarded as exemplary models of developmental states. The core of the developmental state formulation is the pivotal role of the state in development. The developmental state recognises the 'cardinal role of the state as agent of planned growth and transformation' (White and Wade 1988:3). Therefore, the developmental state exists 'when the state possesses the vision, leadership and capacity to bring about a positive transformation of society within a condensed period of time' (Fritz and Menocal 2007:533). Leftwich's definition of developmental states is useful here:

> [T]hose states whose successful economic and social development performance illustrates how their political purposes and institutional structures (especially their bureaucracies) have been developmentally-driven, while their developmental objectives have been politically-driven (2007:12).

Rather than leaving everything to the mercy of the market, the developmental state plays a critical role in 'altering market incentives, reducing risks, offering entrepreneurial visions, and managing conflicts' (Johnson 1999:48). The economy is not left to operate under impersonal and invisible market forces. Rather, the market is 'guided by the conception of a long term national rationality of investment formulated by government officials' (White and Wade 1988:7). For this to obtain, the developmental state needs to have a 'determined developmental elite' (Leftwich 1995:401) who have the vision and stamina to put the country on a developmental path. The developmental elite needs to embrace a 'developmentalist ideology' (Mkandawire 2001) with 'revolutionary social transformation' (Woo-Cumings 1999:7) as its goal and a 'mission ... of ensuring economic development' (Mkandawire 2001:290) and 'larger social objectives' (Huff, Dewitt and Oughton 2001:712).

In addition, the developmental state needs to have some 'relative autonomy' (Leftwich 1995:401) to enable it to adequately carry out the developmentalist mandate. The state must either be from constraining 'social forces' (Mkandawire 2001:290) or, as in the case of developing countries, from donor-stringent conditionalities that would otherwise prevent the state from achieving its developmental mission. The success arising from the latter type of autonomy is what Blessings Chinsinga demonstrates in chapter five in reference to the fertiliser subsidy programme in Malawi. In either case, autonomy enables the state to 'devise long term economic policies unencumbered by the claims of myopic private interests' (Mkandawire 2001:290). Moreover, in order to effectively realise the developmental vision, the developmental state needs a 'powerful, competent and insulated economic bureaucracy' (Leftwich 1995:40) with the capacity to implement policies 'sagaciously and effectively' (Mkandawire 2001:290). The bureaucrats in charge must have a sense of mission, identify themselves with national goals and have position of leadership in society (Onis 1991:114).

While the developmental state may be the necessary path for developing countries to replace the neo-liberal NPM reforms that have failed, the developmental state is not without its problems. There are costs associated with the developmental state that, if not well considered, may lead to disastrous results. As Chang (1999:198) argues, 'making a case for the developmental state does not necessarily mean ignoring the cost associated with active interventionist policies'. The problem with developmental states is that the state elite can 'structure market incentives... to enrich itself and its friends at the expense of customers, good jobs, and development' (Johnson 1999:48). In this way, the developmental state can open the floodgates to corruption, as in Japan and South Korea, for example, where the developmental state model led to 'profound structural corruption with cash flowing from state to business and from business to politicians in truly floodtide dimensions' (Woo-Cumings 1999:10). In South Korea, there were cases of corruption involving 'astronomical sums' of money, $900 million in the case of one former president and $650 million in another (Woo-Cumings 1999:11). Moreover, the developmental state can lead to undemocratic tendencies. In their quest to achieve the developmentalist mission, the developmental elite may be tempted to employ autocratic instruments. As Kwon argues (2005:483), the developmental state has 'shown an affinity with authoritarian politics'. This affinity arises from the fact that 'legitimation occurs from the state's achievement, not from the way it came to power' (Johnson 1999:53). Woo-Cumings (1999:20) gives examples of the 'ugly reality of authoritarianism' in several East Asian states (Woo-Cumings 1999:20).

In addition, the legitimacy issues in developmental states can lead to instability and 'severe crises, such as after Japan's defeat in World War II or the Korean revolution of 1987' (Johnson 1999:53). Moreover, if not well formulated, the developmental state can lead to a widening inequality gap, as the economic growth gained by state interventions may not easily be translated into meaningful transformations of everyday life. For instance, the developmental state in Japan 'strengthened the abstract entity called Japan but has not done much to enrich the lives of Japanese consumers and city dwellers' (Johnson 1999:50). Other arguments against the developmental state include problems of human capital, the possibility of the state crowding out private investment, economies of scale and market imperfections and failures (Mkandawire 2001:292).

The observations highlighted above are important for any developing country seeking to take the developmental state route; they are critical issues that must be taken into consideration if this route is to be a success. Although desirable, the developmental state is 'not an easy combination to put together' (Johnson 1999:60); it is 'impossible to manufacture and not susceptible to any of the more obvious forms of promotion' (Fritz and Menacal 2007:533). In this respect, there are some specific structural and institutional issues in developing countries that may militate against the emergence of the developmental state and hence require a thorough checking. These include dependence and fragmented aid, bribery by foreign companies, lack of coherent ideology, existing neopatrimonial structures, clientelism, the 'softness' of the state and its vulnerability to capture by special interest groups and lack of technical and analytical capacity (Mkandawire 2001:294; Fritz and Menacal 2007:533). It is important that these issues be addressed before embarking on a developmental state model, because 'when [the developmental state] is done properly, it can produce miracles of economic development' (Johnson 1999:60).

Structure of this Volume

The aim of this volume is threefold. The first aim is to provide analytical case-studies on particular public-sector reforms in Malawi. The second is to contribute to the theoretical debates that shape the particular reform components being studied. The third aim, through this combination of practical Malawian case study insights and the theoretical frameworks that flow from them, is to develop generalization about public-sector reform dynamics in developing countries in general, and in Africa in particular. We therefore present four papers that put the theoretical issues we have discussed in this introduction into practical case-study contexts. Each paper analyses a specific reform in the Malawian public sector in line with the core theoretical debates discussed above regarding decentralisation, public-private partnerships, performance contracting and the developmental state.

In chapter two, Asiyati Chiweza presents an analysis of decentralisation dynamics. Her argument is that decentralisation is mainly implemented as a vehicle for achieving greater accountability, efficiency, government responsiveness, participation, sustainable results and democratic ends. For Malawi, Chiweza highlights the fact that the decentralisation programme is aimed at promoting participatory planning, and representative democracy through the election of councillors to the district assemblies. This, in turn, is assumed to lead to more efficient service delivery, accountability, effectiveness and good governance. But for these outcomes to materialise, the Malawian central government was required to devolve functional powers, responsibilities and resources to the local government, while maintaining responsibility for national projects, general policy guidance, monitoring and inspection of local government activities. However, Chiweza reveals that these decentralisation goals are far from being reached. The decentralisation reforms in Malawi have met several challenges that have threatened their effective implementation. For instance, the central government has not been willing in devolve power and responsibilities to the local assemblies. Moreover, those sectors that are said to have been devolved actually exhibit deconcentration than devolution, leading to coordination difficulties. In addition, the government has done very little to ensure a sustainable financial base for the effective functioning of the decentralised structures. Moreover, there is limited accountability and little culture of democratisation; decisions made are not legally binding, and there are few checks and balances. In conclusion, Chiweza highlights the problems of having a multiplicity of objectives that emphasise technocratic ability while leaving out political and social imperatives. She argues that the critical premises of local government have not significantly changed and that the institutions are still fragile, making local government appear to be only an extension of the central government.

Chapter three presents Happy Kayuni's analysis of public-private partnerships (PPPs) in Malawian local assemblies. Kayuni argues that the rationale behind the implementation of PPPs as a component of public-sector reform is to ensure better service delivery, cut service-delivery costs, increase public participation in service delivery and achieve greater accountability and transparency. However for these objectives to be met, certain preconditions have to prevail. These conditions include predictability in the legal and regulatory environment, open and competitive procurement processes, well-researched and prepared transactions, government commitment, a mature financial sector and stakeholder support. However, in Malawi, these preconditions are not yet present and, as a result, the PPPs do not achieve the intended outcomes. In particular, there is a lack of coordination, leading to duplication of tasks and overconcentration of PPPs in a few assemblies. Kayuni observes that misunderstandings abound concerning the role of PPPs. In addition, due to capacity problems at the local government level, many NGOs that are supposed to form partnerships with local assemblies tend to circumvent the decentralised planning framework, thereby crippling the partnerships. This problem is exacerbated by the perception that assemblies are risky partners due to their poor financial base, administrative constraints, inadequate supervision of partners' programmes and political interference and corruption. Kayuni further finds that the Malawian business environment is not equipped to provide effective PPP partners. In conclusion, Kayuni underscores the importance of solid institutional frameworks to support PPPs. In his analysis, Malawian local assemblies do not currently possess such frameworks.

Similar conclusions are drawn by Richard Tambulasi in chapter four, where he analyses the dynamics of NPM performance contracting in Malawi. Tambulasi notes that NPM-based performance contract measures were put in place in order to create staffing structures and management systems that would enable ministries and departments to achieve their objectives effectively and efficiently. However, like all NPM tools, performance-based contracting is context-specific, and Tambulasi argues that Malawi does not have a conducive environment for the effective implementation of performance contracting, hence the failure of the system and its abandonment seven years after implementation. According to Tambulasi, the problems that led to the failure of performance contracting in Malawi include its swift adoption before putting in place the necessary institutional frameworks, lack of clear performance targets and lack of financial resources to sustain the system. It appears the government was not committed, as managers lacked sufficient control and promotions were based on long-term service and political allegiance rather than merit. Due the increased financial remunerations of staff on contract, the scheme was used as a political instrument for patronage to manipulate the bureaucracy for political gain rather than as a system for achieving greater efficiency. Tambulasi concludes that performance-based contracting is not a magic key that solves all performance problems regardless of country-specific situations.

In the final chapter, Blessings Chinsinga introduces the developmental state as a possible cure for the problems brought about by donor-driven neo-liberal reforms. Using the overwhelmingly successful 2005/2006 fertiliser subsidy programme in Malawi, which the government embarked on despite donors' unwillingness to support, as a case study, Chinsinga demonstrates that the developmental potential of the Malawian state can lead to higher levels of developmental goals if replicated in other sectors of the economy. Malawi implemented the fertiliser subsidy programme despite lack of support from the international donor community. However, the success of the programme made the donors change their anti-subsidy orientation and follow the government line, commissioning studies to draw lessons from the experience and later giving their support for the government-initiated subsidy programme. Donor agencies rose above their often ideologically driven policy narratives for a meaningful trade-off with the prevailing realities of the Malawian context. In his analysis, Chinsinga shows that the positive results of the programme demonstrate the positive developmental consequences of state autonomy from donors and public legitimacy. In conclusion, Chinsinga recommends that, for the lessons from the fertiliser subsidy to be replicated to other sectors, the political elites have to get developmental politics right while, at the same time, building policy-making technical capacity.

Future Perspectives on the Study of Public-sector Reforms in Africa

To conclude, this paper seeks to make some suggestions on future research perspectives on public-sector reforms in Africa in general. This is in no way designed to serve as an exhaustive prescription for how public-sector reforms in Africa should be studied but only as a suggestion on some pertinent methodological and theoretical issues that may be taken into account in the analysis of the dynamics of public-sector reforms in the future. In this way, I hope to create new research grounds for further analysis of public sector reform.

The literature on public-sector reforms in Africa is diverse and multidisciplinary. The richness of this research is that it brings out various case studies that provide rich information and insights on the nature and dynamics of public sector reforms. On the other hand, the major weakness of the literature is that it does not have a unified theoretical and methodological ground from which further research questions can be formulated, and lessons and hypotheses drawn. Most of the current literature merely tells stories about public-sector reforms in Africa without making an attempt towards theory building. The analytical and causal accounts of public-sector reforms in Africa are still focused on the ideological, doctrinal and rhetorical aspects of the reforms. Although such accounts are helpful in understanding the dynamics of public-sector reform in Africa, they do not fully bring out its intricacies. There is need to go beyond narrative to explore the institutional, political and organisational dynamics that shape public-sector reforms and that result in unsustainable outcomes. Alternative theoretical and analytical frameworks that can help to achieve this deeper analysis are available. These include the use of new-institutionalism theories, organisational theories, international relations theories, political theories and related theoretical frameworks. For practical reasons, it is not possible in this article to illustrate how all of these theories might shape the study of public-sector reforms in Africa. Such an exercise would require another publication of its own. I will therefore focus here on only one theoretical perspective – the new institutionalism – for the further study of public sector reforms in Africa. The new institutionalism is particularly important, as 'institutions have always been regarded as the basic building blocks of social and political life' (DiMaggio and Powell 1991:3).

The New Institutionalism: Theoretical Perspective

New institutionalism can provide a conceptual framework for the analysis of public-sector reforms in Africa that can create new grounds for formulating research questions and drawing hypotheses. From this perspective, institutions are crucial for understanding the dynamics of public-sector reform processes in Africa. By institution, I do not refer to organisations, as implied in some public-sector reform literature (see, for instance, Economic Commission for Africa 2005). Rather I mean all the formal and informal 'rules of the game' or, as North puts it (1990:3), the 'humanly devised constraints that shape human interaction'. Institutions in this sense must be distinguished from organisations. While institutions are the 'rules of the game', organisations are the players (North 1990:4). The focal pillars of new-institutionalist explanations are actors' preferences and institutions. Institutions not only shape actors' strategies but their goals as well. By mediating their relations of cooperation and conflict, institutions structure political situations and leave their own imprint on political and public- sector reform outcomes (Bulmer 1994:425). Institutional explanations of public-sector reforms examine the ways in which institutions structure 'incentives, instantiate norms, define roles, prescribe or proscribe behaviour, or procedurally channel politics so as to alter political outcomes relative to what would have occurred in the absence of (or under alternative) institutions' (Jupille and Caporaso 1999:431). The new institutionalism literature is divided into five main orientations: sociological, historical, empirical, rational choice and international (see Peters 2005). Any of these 'schools' of institutionalism could be used in the analysis of public-sector reforms, but, for practical purposes, I will focus on how the sociological and the historical versions of new institutionalism offer a possible theoretical framework for analyzing public-sector reforms in Africa.

Sociological Institutionalism: Institutional Isomorphism

Sociological institutionalism can be used to analyse and understand the mechanisms and forces that make African countries adopt reforms from donor organisations or other countries. In particular, the institutional isomorphism variant of sociological institutionalism (see DiMaggio and Powell 1991) can be used to analyse the mechanisms that trigger public-sector reforms in Africa. The institutional isomorphism perspective focuses on 'forces pressing communities towards accommodation with the outside world' (DiMaggio and Powell 1991:66). The institutional isomorphic mechanisms include 'coercive', 'mimetic' and 'normative' pressures (DiMaggio and Powell 1991:67). Coercive isomorphic pressures are caused by both 'formal and informal pressures exerted on organisations by other organisations upon which they are dependent' (DiMaggio and Powell 1991:67). In most instances, with coercive pressures, public-sector reforms become a condition of 'economic resources' (Radaelli 2000:29) or 'approval for lower level jurisdiction' (Roy and Seguin 2000). Coercive isomorphic pressures could therefore explain the role of donors in many public-sector reform initiatives in Africa. For example, the use of financial conditionalities is clearly a coercive isomorphic pressure.

Mimetic isomorphic processes result from imitation due to uncertainty (DiMaggio and Powell 1991:69). Through this mechanism, owing to uncertainty in the environment, countries tend to model their reforms on those countries that are seen to be more successful or legitimate in achieving policy objectives. From this perspective, one could explore uncertainties in the political, economical, technological and sociological environments that lead to public-sector reforms and the characteristics of the countries on which the reforms are modelled. Lastly, with normative isomorphic pressures, public-sector reforms are thought to occur due to an 'increased consensus among an increasingly unified policy community on the appropriateness of particular ways of working' (Lodge 2002:48). This perspective emphasises the role of policy networks and epistemic communities in public-sector reform processes. An epistemic community is a 'network of professionals with recognised expertise and competence in a particular domain and an authoritative claim to policy-relevant knowledge within that domain or issue' (Haas 1992:3). Such communities are instrumental in giving public-sector reform advice to countries, as they are producers of policy-reform knowledge that can be transferred. On the other hand, policy networks are non-hierarchical and interdependent relationships that link a variety of actors who have common interests with regard to a policy and who exchange resources to pursue these shared interests (Borzel 1998:254). These policy networks are institutionalised contacts that exist at national and international level. Epistemic communities and policy networks can operate at both the national or international level. However, owing to globalisation processes, most national-level epistemic communities and policy networks have membership or affiliation at the international level and vice versa.

Historical Institutionalism

Along with sociological institutionalism, historical institutionalism can be used in the analysis of reform processes at national level, either through the use of single case studies or comparative studies. Specifically, historical institutionalism can be used to understand how country-specific institutional dynamics shape public-sector reform processes and outcomes over time. This perspective is historical because it recognises that public-sector reform 'must be understood as a process that unfolds over time' (Pierson 1996:126). An important aspect of historical institutionalism is that it has a 'particularly encompassing interpretation of the role of institutions' (Bulmer 1998:370) in public-sector reform processes. For instance, historical institutionalism can be used to analyse how public-sector reforms are constrained or facilitated by existing institutional frameworks. In this regard, historical institutionalism contributes to the understanding of why reforms have different consequences given the same institutional framework (for single case studies) or different institutional frameworks (for comparative case studies). The aim is to use historical institutionalism to examine whether public-sector reforms have resulted in the planned results or in unintended consequences. Historical institutionalism tells us that 'unintended consequences are likely and widespread' (Pierson 1996:136) in reform processes. Historical institutionalism argues that reforms are path-dependent; it 'rejects the traditional postulate that the same operative forces will generate the same results everywhere in favour of the view that the effect of such forces will be mediated by the contextual features of a given situation often inherited from the past' (Hall and Taylor 1996:941). Moreover, organisations are 'recalcitrant tools, and efforts to direct them yield unanticipated consequences beyond anyone's control' (DiMaggio and Powell 1991:14). Path dependence 'means that history matters' (North 1990:102). It implies that historical institutionalism is 'more sensitive to historical legacies, cultural contexts, with the relations of power, with the 'stickiness' of institutions or their path dependent proclivity' (Leftwich 2007:46). In terms of public-sector reform processes, path dependence could help in understanding why some reform projects fail. According to Peters (2005:20), reforms are 'path dependent and once launched on that path they will persist in that pattern until some significant force intervenes to divert them from the established direction'. Reforms fail because old ways of operating 'can become so institutionalised and historically embedded that it becomes nearly impossible to break free from the established path' (Greener 2002:164). In this regard, path dependence could explain why public-sector reforms based on the neo-liberal formula in Africa fail and why there are calls for the return of the developmental state. This operational path can, of course, be changed but only with much difficulty. It would require a 'good deal of political pressure to produce that change' (Peters 2005:71). What is central in this perspective, therefore, is understanding the 'logic of appropriateness that shapes individuals' actions within institutions (Bulmer 1998:375), thereby informing reform outcomes. The vitality of the logic of appropriateness in explaining public-sector reforms lies in the selectivity of country-specific institutions in adopting particular reform options. The argument is that institutional imperatives embedded in the 'logic of appropriateness …constrain the limits of acceptable action of government' (Peters 2005:75).

References

Ademolekun, L., Kulemeka N., Laleye, M., 1997, 'Political Transition, Economic Liberalization and Civil Service Reform in Malawi', *Public Administration and Development,* Vol. 17, pp. 209-222.

Bangura, Y. and Larbi, G.A., 2006, 'Introduction: Globalisation and Public Sector Reform', in Y. Bangura, Y and G.A. Larbi, eds., *Public Sector Reform in Developing Countries,* New York: Palgrave.

Batley R. and Larbi, G., 2004, *The Changing Role of Government: The Reform of the Public Services in Developing Countries,* New York: Palgrave.

Borzel, T., 1998, 'Organising Babylon: On the Different Conceptions of Policy Networks', *Public Administration,* Vol 76, pp. 253-73.

Bulmer, S., 1994, 'Institutions and Policy Change in the European Communities: The Case of Merger Control', *Public Administration ,* Vol. 72, pp. 423-444.

Bulmer, S., 1998, 'New Institutionalism and the Governance of the Single European Market', *Journal of European Public Policy,* Vol. 5. No 3, pp. 365-386.

Chang, H., 1999, 'The Economic Theory of the Developmental State', in M. Woo-Cumings, ed., *The Developmental State,* New York: Cornell University Press.

Chinsinga, B., 2005, 'District Assemblies in a Fix: The Perils of the Politics of Capacity in the Political and Administrative Reforms in Malawi', *Development Southern Africa,* Vol. 22, No. 4, pp. 529-548.

Christensen, T., and Laegreid, P., 2001, 'New Public Management: The Effects of Contractualism and Devolution on Political Control', *Public Management Review,* Vol. 3, No. 1, pp. 73 -94.

Common, R.K., 1998, 'Convergence and Transfer: A Review of the Globalisation of New Public Management', *International Journal of Public Sector Management,* Vol. 11, No. 6, pp. 440-450.

Common, R.K., 2001, *Public Management and Policy Transfer in Southeast Asia,* Ashgate: Aldershot.

DiMaggio, P.J. and Powell, W.W., 1991, 'The Iron Cage Revisited: Institutional Isomorphism and Collective Rationality in Organisational Fields', in W.W Powell and P.J. DiMaggio, eds., *The New Institutionalism in Organisational Analysis,* Chicago: University of Chicago Press, pp. 63–82.

Dolowitz, D. P., and Marsh D., 2000, 'Learning From Abroad: The Role of Policy Transfer in Contemporary Policy Making', *Governance: An International Journal of Policy and Administration,* Vol. 13, No. 1, pp. 5-24.

Dunleavy, P. and Margetts, H., 2000, 'The Advent of Digital Government: Public Bureaucracies and the State in the Internet Age', Paper presented at the annual conference of the American Political Science Association, Washington DC, 4 September.

Economic Commission for Africa, 2005, *Public Sector Management Reform in Africa,* Addis Ababa: Economic Commission for Africa.

Evans, M., 2004: *Policy Transfer in a Global Perspective,* Ashgate: Aldershot.

Evans, P.B., 1989, 'Predatory, Developmental, and Other Apparatuses: A Comparative Political Economy Perspective on the Third World State', *Sociological Forum,* Vol. 4, No. 4, pp. 561-587.

Flinders, M., 2005, 'The Politics of Public–Private Partnerships', *British Journal of Politics and International Relations,* Vol 7, pp. 215–239.

Fritz, V. and Menocal, A., 2007, 'Developmental States in the New Millennium: Concepts and Challenges for a New Aid Agenda', *Development Policy Review,* Vol. 25, No. 5, pp. 531-552.

Goldsmith, M.J. and Page, E.C., 1997, 'Farewell to the British State?', in J. Lane, ed., *Public Sector Reform: Rationale, Trends and Problems,* London, Sage.

Greener, I., 2002, 'Understanding NHS Reform: The Policy-Transfer, Social Learning, and Path Dependence Perspectives', *Governance: An International Journal of Policy, Administration, and Institutions,* Vol. 15, No. 2, pp. 161-183.

Haas, P. M., 1992, 'Introduction: Epistemic Communities and International Policy Coordination, *International Organisation,* Vol. 46, No. 1, pp. 1-35.

Hall, P.A. and Taylor, R.C.R., 1996, 'Political Science and the Three New Institutionalisms', *Political Studies,* Vol. 44, pp. 936-957.

Halligan, J., 1997, 'New Public Sector Models: Reform in Australia and New Zealand', in J. Lane, ed., *Public Sector Reform: Rationale, Trends and Problems,* London, Sage.

Haque, M. S, 2001, 'The Diminishing Publicness of Public Services under the Current Mode of Governance', *Public Administration Review,* Vol. 61, No. 1, pp. 65-82.

Hirschmann, D., 1993, 'Institutional Development in the Era of Economic Policy Reform: Concerns, Contradictions, and Illustrations from Malawi', *Public Administration and Development,* Vol. 13, No. 2, pp. 113–28.

Hodge, G. A., 2004, 'The Risky Business of Public–Private Partnerships', *Australian Journal of Public Administration,* Vol. 63, No. 4, pp. 37–49.

Hood, C., 1991, 'A Public Management for all Seasons?', *Public Administration,* Vol 69, pp. 3-19.

Hope, K.R., Sr. and Chikulo, B.C., 2000, 'Decentralisation, The New Public Management and the Changing Role of the Public Sector in Africa', *Public Management: An International Journal of Research And Theory,* Vol. 2, No.1. pp. 25-42.

Hoque, Z., 2005, 'Securing Institutional Legitimacy or Organisational Effectiveness? A Case Examining the Impact of Public Sector Reform Initiatives in an Australian Local Authority', *International Journal of Public Sector Management,* Vol. 18, No. 4, pp. 367-382.

Huff, W.G., Dewitt, G. and Oughton, C., 2001, 'Credibility and Reputation Building in Developmental States: A Model with East Asian Application', *World Development* Vol. 29, No. 4, pp. 711-721.

Hughes, O.H., 1998, *Public Management and Administration: An Introduction,* 2nd ed., New York: Palgrave.

Hussein, M.K., 2003, 'The Role of Malawian Local Government in Community Development', *Development Southern Africa*, Vol. 20, No. 2, pp. 271- 282.

Jamali, D., 2004, 'A Public-Private Partnership in the Lebanese Telecommunications Industry: Critical Success Factors and Policy Lessons', *Public Works Management and Policy*, Vol. 9, No. 2, pp. 103-119.

Johnson, C, 1999, 'The Developmental State: Odyssey of a Concept', in M. Woo-Cumings, ed, *The Developmental State*, New York: Cornell University Press.

Jupille. J. and Caporaso, J.A., 1999, 'Institutionalism and the European Union: Beyond International Relations and Comparative Politics', *Annual Review of Political Science*, Vol. 2, pp. 429- 444.

Kickert, W.J.M., 1997, 'Anglo-Saxon Public Management and European Governance: The Case of Dutch Administrative Reforms', in J. Lane, ed, *Public Sector Reform: Rationale, Trends and Problems*, London: Sage.

Koppenjan, J.F.M., 2005, 'The Formation of Public-Private Partnerships: Lessons from Nine Transport Infrastructure Projects in the Netherlands', *Public Administration*, Vol. 83, No. 1, pp. 135–157.

Kwon, H., 2005, 'Transforming the Developmental Welfare State in East Asia', *Development and Change*, Vol. 36, No. 3, pp. 477–497.

Lane, J., 1997, 'Introduction: Public Sector Reform: Only Deregulation, Privatisation and Marketisation?', in J. Lane, ed., *Public Sector Reform: Rationale, Trends and Problems*, London, Sage.

Lane, J., 1999, 'Contractualism in the Public Sector', *Public Management Review*, Vol. 1, No. 2, pp. 179 -194.

Larbi, G.A., 1999, *The New Public Management Approach and Crisis States*, UNRISD Discussion Paper No 112, Geneva: UNRISD.

Larbi G.A, 2006, 'Applying the New Public Management in Developing Countries', in Y. Bangura and G.A. Larbi, eds, *Public Sector Reform in developing Countries*, New York: Palgrave.

Leftwich, A., 1995, 'Bringing Politics Back In: Towards a Model of the Developmental State', *Journal of Development Studies*, Vol. 31, No. 3, pp. 400-427.

Leftwich, A., 2007, *The Political Approach to Institutional Formation, Maintenance and Change: A Literature Review Essay*, IGGG Discussion Paper Series Number Fourteen October, University of York.

Li, B., Akintoye, A., Edwards P.J. and Hardcastle, C., 2005, 'Critical Success Factors for PPP/PFI Projects in the UK Construction Industry', *Construction Management and Economics*, Vol. 23 No. 5, pp. 459-471.

Lodge, M., 2002, 'Varieties of Europeanization and the National Regulatory State', *Public Policy and Administration*, Vol. 17, No. 2, pp. 43-67.

Metcalfe L. and Richards S., 1990, *Improving Public Management*, London: Sage.

Mhone, G., 1992, 'The Political Economy of Malawi: An Overview', in G Mhone, ed., *Malawi at the Crossroads: The Postcolonial Political Economy*, Harare, SAPES.

Mhone, G., 2003, 'Developmentalism and the Role of the State', Paper prepared for the Workshop on Growth And Development, Premier's Policy Development Unit, Kwa Zulu Natal Provincial Government, February.

Mimba, N., Helden, G.J. and Tellema, S., 2007, 'Public Sector Performance Measurements in Developing Countries: A Literature Review and Research Agenda', *Journal of Accounting and Organisational Change*, Vol. 3. No. 3, pp. 193-208.

Minogue, M., 2002, 'Power to the People? Good Governance and the Reshaping of the State', in U. Kothari and M. Minogue, eds., *Development Theory and Practice: Critical Perspectives*, London, Palgrave.

Mkandawire, T., 2001, 'Thinking about Developmental States in Africa', *Cambridge Journal of Economics*, Vol. 24, pp. 289-313.

Mxakato-Diseko, N. J., 2008, 'The Changing Role and Image of the Public Sector in Africa', Paper presented at the Workshop for Enhancing Leadership Capacity Development, African Public Service Commissions, Kampala, 6-11 April.

North, D., 1990, *Institutions, Institutional Change and Economic Performance*, Cambridge: Cambridge University Press.

Olowu, D., 1990. 'The Failure of Current Decentralisation Programmes in Africa', in J.S. Wunsch and D. Olowu, eds., *The Failure of the Centralized State*, Boulder CO: Westview Press, pp. 74-99.

Onis, Z., 1991, 'Review Article: The Logic of the Developmental State, *Comparative Politics*, Vol. 24, No. 1, pp. 109-126.

Ontario Federation of Labour, 2005, 'Private Public Partnerships and the Transformation'. (http://www.ofl.ca/uploads/library/policy_papers/P3s.pdf). 15 July 2008.

Osborne, D., and Gaebler, T., 1992, *Reinventing Government: How the Entrepreneurial Spirit is Transforming Government*, Oxford, Oxford University Press.

Peters, B.G., 2005, Institutional Theory in Political Science: The New Institutionalism, 2nd Edition, London: Continuum.

Pierson, P., 1996, 'The Path to European Integration: A Historical Institutionalist Analysis', *Comparative Political Studies*, Vol. 29, No. 2, pp. 123-163.

Polidano, C., 1998, 'Introduction: New Public Management, Old Hat?', *Journal of International Development*, Vol. 10, pp. 373-375.

Polidano, C., 2001, 'Why Civil Service Reforms Fail', *Public Management Review*, Vol. 3, pp. 345–361.

Pollitt, C. and Bouckaert, G., 2000, *Public Management Reform: A Comparative Analysis*, Oxford: Oxford University Press.

Radaelli, C., 2000, 'Policy Transfer in the European Union: Institutional Isomorphism as a Source of Legitimacy', *Governance: An International Journal of Policy and Administration*, Vol. 13, No. 1, pp. 25-43.

Roy, C., and Seguin, F., 2000, 'The Institutionalization of Efficiency-Oriented Approaches for Public Service Improvement', *Public Productivity and Management Review*, Vol. 23, No. 4, pp. 449-468.

Smoke, P., 2003, 'Decentralisation in Africa: Goals, Dimensions, Myths and Challenges', *Public Administration and Development*, Vol. 23, pp. 7-16.

Steunenburg, B. and Mol, M., 1997, 'Fiscal and Financial Decentralisation: A Comparative Analysis of Six West European Countries', in J. Lane, ed., *Public Sector Reform: Rationale, Trends and Problems*, London, Sage.

Tambulasi, R.I.C., 2007, 'Who is Fooling Who? New Public Management Oriented Management Accounting and Political Control in Malawi's Local Governance', *Journal of Accounting and Organisational Change*, Vol. 3, No. 3, pp. 302-328.

Tambulasi, R.I.C. and Kayuni, H.K., 2007a, 'Public Sector Reform in Malawi', in N. Patel and R. Lasvasen, eds., *Government and Politics in Malawi*, Blantyre: Montfort Press.

Tambulasi, R.I.C. and Kayuni, H.K., 2007b, 'Decentralisation Opening a New Window for Corruption: An Accountability Assessment of Malawi's Four Years of Democratic Local Governance', *Journal of Asian and African Studies,* Vol. 42. No. 2, pp. 163–183.

Therkildesen, O., 2001, *Efficiency, Accountability and Implementation: Public Sector Reform in East and Southern Africa*, Geneva: UNRISD.

Turner, M. and Hulme, D., 1997, *Governance, Administration and Development: Making the State Work*, London: Macmillan.

United Nations, 2001, *World Public Sector Report: Globalisation and the State*, New York: United Nations.

White G. and Wade R., 1988, 'Developmental States and Markets in East Asia: An Introduction', in G. White and R. Wade, eds., *Developmental States in East Asia*, London: Macmillan, pp. 1-29.

Woo-Cumings, M., 1999, 'Introduction: Chalmers Johnson and the Politics of Nationalism and Development', in M. Woo-Cumings, ed., *The Developmental State,* New York: Cornell University Press.

Zhang, X., 2005, 'Critical Success Factors for Public-Private Partnerships in Infrastructure Development', *Journal of Construction Engineering and Management*, Vol. 131, No. 1, pp. 3-14.

2

Public-sector Reforms and Decentralisation of Public Services: Lessons From Malawi (1994-2006)

Asiyati Lorraine Chiweza

Introduction

Since the 1980s, African countries have been making huge efforts to improve the performance of the public sector through various reform initiatives. Anchored by the new public management (NPM) paradigm and demands for good governance, the reform initiatives have sought to reduce the core functions of the state, foster fiscal stability, emphasise managerial efficiency within the public sector, redefine relations between public and private sectors, promote public accountability, improve service delivery, reduce corruption and change values and attitudes. Post-colonial African states built upon systems inherited from the colonisers (Tordoff and Young 1994; Mukwena and Lolojih 2002; Therkildsen 2001). Thus, in the immediate post-independence period, most African states focused on building public administrations that could spearhead national development, motivated by the conviction that statism was the best way to promote development. As a result, expansion of the role of government in many spheres, together with Weberian approaches emphasising procedural and instrumental approaches to the organisation of public administration apparatuses, dominated immediate post-colonial reform initiatives (Mhone 2003). Not surprisingly, earlier decentralisation reforms, shaped in the mould of the colonial age, more commonly boosted central control in their design as well as operation (Chiweza 2005; Tordoff and Young 1994; Mawhood 1993).

Over time, although reform agendas varied, reforms have generally been seen as a means to bring about desired changes in the public sector and improve its capacity as well as performance (Siddiquee 2006). A number of researchers point out that, among other imperatives, current reforms are mainly driven by economic crises and the need for structural adjustment, donor demands, the perceived failure of the African public sector to promote sustainable development and the "third wave" of democratisation and political changes taking place in many African countries (Batley 1999; Mhone 2003; Mkandawire and Soludo 1999; Mukwena and Lolojih 2002; Schacter 2000; Therkildsen 2001). Therkildsen (2001) notes that, despite differences in design and emphasis, many of the current reform initiatives are inspired by NPM approaches, and the official reform language across the southern and eastern African region has been strikingly similar. Broadly speaking, the NPM approach emphasises transformation of the public sector by reducing its core functions, fostering fiscal stability, emphasising managerial efficiency, redefining relations between public and private sectors, promoting public accountability, improving service delivery, reducing corruption and changing values and attitudes.

Public sector Reforms in Malawi

Public-sector institutional development in Malawi reflects a point of reference in British parliamentary and government institutions. Thus, the very first efforts at public-sector reform in Malawi were embarked on immediately after the attainment of independence (Duverall 2001). A major concern at the time was how to manage the transition from an expatriate-based civil service to one dominated by Africans. However, since the early 1990s, Malawi has embarked on a quite different reform project within its public sector. This is being done as part of the governance improvement process that began with changes in the national political system that took place in 1994 (Government of Malawi 2002). In particular, the election of a democratic government in 1994 and the introduction of a new structural adjustment programme in 1995 with broad-based support from the donor community provided an impetus for many of the public-sector reform efforts that the country has been undertaking. During the 1990s, a number of policy reviews and programmes directed at reforming the public sector were attempted, often simultaneously. Among them were the public-sector management review, civil-service pay and employment study, civil-service action plan, the poverty alleviation programme, functional reviews of the ministries, decentralisation and formation of local-government policy reform, medium-term expenditure framework and sector investment programmes (Duverall, 2001). The public-service management reform programme (PSRP) aims at developing a public service that is efficient, effective and responsive to national aspirations and facilitates the eradication of poverty (Government of Malawi 2002:9).

This paper focuses on decentralisation as one of the reform initiatives Malawi has implemented. It examines the nature, direction and quality of the reform and asks whether the it has the potential of fostering greater efficiency and accountability in public-service delivery. The paper starts by discussing the concept of decentralisation, because the way the term is conceptualised and understood has a bearing on the nature of reform. A brief historical background follows this discussion, in view of the fact that current decentralisation reforms have their origins in previous reform efforts. Thereafter, the paper discusses the nature and direction of the current decentralisation reforms, offers an empirical analysis of the reforms and concludes with a summary of the whole discussion.

The Concept of Decentralisation

In the discourse of public-sector reforms in Africa, the term "decentralisation" has a variety of meanings, and what is meant by decentralisation in the literature is even more varied. Generally, decentralisation is understood as a process whereby power and responsibilities are transferred from a central authority to lower levels in a territorial hierarchy (Cook and Manor 1998; Manhood 1993). It is closely linked to the concept of subsidiarity, which states that the most effective govern-ance of any organisation occurs when authority for decision-making is located as close as possible to where actions take place. It follows that functions need be devolved to the lowest level of social order that is capable of completing them (McGinn and Welch 1999; Stohr 2001). Mawhood (1993) notes that decentralisa-tion suggests the hope of cracking open the blockages of an inert central bureauc-racy, curing managerial constipation and giving more direct access to the people.

However, in practice, decentralisation is a broader term and can take different forms and mean different things to different people (Bardhan 2002; Mawhood 1993). In a review of African decentralisation, Ribot (2002) shows that there is considerable confusion and obfuscation about what constitutes decentralisation. He argues that, in the name of decentralisation, powers are being allocated to a variety of bodies, actors and authorities that may not have sufficient powers and may not be downwardly accountable. Decentralisation is also applied to pro-grammes and reforms that are ultimately designed to retain central control (Conyers 2000; Mawhood 1993). Therefore, understanding what the concept means in each particular context is important because the style and approach of decentrali-sation adopted by a country holds ramifications for the potential of any decen-tralisation reforms to achieve their stated objectives (Grant 2002).

During the colonial period, decentralisation focused more on management of local populations by extending central administration into the local arena (Mamdani 1996). In most cases, this constituted a transfer of power to tradi-tional authorities under the direct control of the central colonial government. This was reinforced by the post-independence period's dominance by one-party states that did not create space for elected local government (Ribot 2002). How-ever, the decentralisation initiatives that most African countries attempted after independence and in the early 1980s centred on public provisioning of services, national cohesion and, to a lesser extent, the voluntary sector. During this period, decentralisation was mainly conceptualised as the transfer of responsibility for planning, management and resource raising and allocation from the central government and its agencies to field units of government ministries or agencies, subordinate units or levels of government, semi-autonomous public authorities or corporations, area-wide, regional or functional authorities or non-governmental, private or voluntary organisations (Cheema and Rondinelli, cited in UNDP 1998:1).

Ideologically, such initiatives were mainly associated with liberal interventionists who regarded decentralisation as an effective means to make government more efficient in development administration (Oakely 1991). Viewed from this perspective, decentralisation becomes a public policy instrument for development administration that seeks to strengthen local governing bodies for quick and efficient implementation of various development schemes. Decentralisation is defined in terms of redistribution of the administrative responsibilities of the central government on the basis of normative liberal assumptions (Gurukkal 2000). In this context, decentralisation takes three basic organisational forms: *deconcentration* of administration to field offices of the central government, *delegation* to semi-autonomous bodies such as parastatals and *devolution* of functions to non-government institutions (Cheema and Rondinelli 1983).

However, as the need for consumer responsiveness in an environment of increased demand for public services rose on the international agenda starting in the late 1980s, a monetarist discourse of decentralisation emerged in which emphasis shifted away from public services towards market mechanisms (Slater 1989). This discourse, largely promoted by the major lenders such as the World Bank, viewed decentralisation as a means of breaking the power of central ministries, increasing revenue generation and shifting the burden of service delivery onto local stakeholders (Mohan and Stokke 2000). The sixth World Bank Report explicitly links decentralisation with market reforms as part of a broader market surrogate strategy geared towards economising scarce administrative resources (World Bank 1983). Accordingly, the organisational forms of decentralisation began to emphasise privatisation and deregulation in addition to deconcentration and devolution. Mohan and Stokke (2000) argue that underpinning this monetarist view is rational choice theory, which permits the more political readings of decentralisation to be transformed into a narrative of capital and efficiency. This resulted in greater emphasis being given to efficiency and incentive discourses that required communities to use their local resources such as labour and other materials as local contributions towards implementation of development projects (Rose 2003). These views present the logic of the market as natural, and they tend to divert attention from issues of political power and the conflicts that inevitably arise when decentralisation changes the distribution of power.

Since the 1990s, decentralisation has been linked into a discourse that combines ideas of collective empowerment and democracy. This is a very different inflection from the liberal interventionist and monetarist approaches that see decentralisation as a means of accelerating state-driven development and economising scarce administrative resources. It has grown 'out of the failure of marketising reforms to significantly reduce absolute poverty' (Houtzager 2003:1) and the rise of good governance and institutions towards the centre stage of the development discourse in the 1990s. It is based on the assumption that pluralism and good governance will make African managers more responsive and better managers of their economies (Chikulo 1997). This approach emphasises reforming state institutions to enhance opportunities for democratisation and poverty reduction. Within this context, decentralisation of power to local government institutions is seen as a means of promoting a new communitarian spirit and forming the seedbed of democratic practice (Mohan and Stokke 2000). Associated with radical populists, this variant of decentralisation entails democratic redistribution of political power to the grassroots (Grukkal 2000). Thus, in the recent wave of decentralisation, the language of reform has shifted to a discourse, currently termed "democratic decentralisation", more focused on democratisation, pluralism and human rights (Cook and Manor 1998; United Nations Capital Development Fund 2000). Donor agencies and theorists now promote democratic decentralisation, involving the establishment of autonomous and independent units of local government, as the ideal form of decentralisation (United Nations Capital Development Fund 2000:4).

Given this background – and the fluidity of the concept of decentralisation – two broad classifications are evident in the literature. Most analysts distinguish among three types of decentralisation: administrative, fiscal and political (Smoke 2003), and four major forms of decentralisation: devolution, deconcentration, delegation and privatisation (Work 2002). However, in seeking to understand decentralisation the pertinent issue that relates to these classifications is to look at what characteristics distinguish the various types and forms of decentralisation.

Administrative decentralisation refers to the transfer of decision-making authority, resources and responsibilities for the delivery of a selected number of public services from the central government to other levels of government, agencies or field offices of government ministries (Mawhood 1993). Deconcentration and delegation are forms of administrative decentralisation. Political decentralisation refers to situations where political power and authority are transferred to sub-national levels of government. Litvack, Ahmad and Bird (1998) argue that political decentralisation occurs when citizens and their elected representatives are involved in public decision-making and contribute to the creation of spaces for participation that can enable and encourage citizen mobilisation. Thus, the most obvious manifestations of this type of decentralisation are elected and empowered sub-national forms of government from village councils to state-level bodies (Work 2002).

Finally, fiscal decentralisation refers to the transfer of financial resources from higher levels to sub-national levels of government (Work 2002). While some analysts consider fiscal decentralisation as a separate type of decentralisation, in many cases it constitutes a cross-cutting element of both administrative and political decentralisation rather than a separate category (Agrawal and Ribot 1999; Oyugi 2000). Furthermore, Barnett, Minis and VanSant (1997) argue that these three aspects should not be viewed as distinct types of decentralisation but need to be looked at as dimensions of decentralisation that reflect increasing and often sequential stages of progress in achieving the governance objectives of decentralisation. These stages entail, first, transfer of functional responsibilities (administrative), then access to resources (fiscal) and, finally, promotion of accountability (political).

Of the four forms of decentralisation, the most commonly discussed in the literature are deconcentration and devolution. The issue of privatisation (including deregulation) as decentralisation is now a contested view, with scholars such as Agrawal and Ribot (1999) arguing that privatisation is not a form of decentralisation because it operates on an exclusive logic rather than an inclusive, public logic of decentralisation. Others, such as Oyugi (2000), argue that privatisation entails a horizontal transfer from public to private and non-profit firms and not a downward transfer, which is what decentralisation is all about. On the other hand, delegation relates to transfer of public functions to lower levels of government, public corporations or any other authority outside of the regular political administrative structure to implement programmes on behalf of a government agency (Ostrom, Schoeder and Wynne 1993).

Deconcentration relates to the transfer of power and responsibilities to local branches of the central state, whereby the central government does not give up any authority but simply relocates its officers to different levels within the national territory (Blair 2000; Crook and Manor 1998; Oyugi 2001; Rondinelli, McCullough and Johnson 1989). In this case, local entities act largely as agents of central government, and the entities maintain the same hierarchical level of accountability to the central ministry or agency rather than to representatives of a local community. On the other hand, devolution is considered a form of political decentralisation and refers to the full transfer of responsibility, decision-making and local revenue generation to a local public authority that is autonomous (Work 2002). It implies the ceding of power and responsibilities to political actors and institutions at lower levels (Crook and Manor 1998).

Closely related to devolution is another variant of decentralisation known as "democratic decentralisation". This form of decentralisation has gained significant attention in recent years, particularly with the onset of democratisation. Democratic decentralisation is viewed as a form of political decentralisation, but one that is linked to and informed by democratic principles. According to Mayo (1960:60), 'a major defining principle of a democratic system is that decision makers are under the effective popular control of the people they are meant to govern'. Therefore, for decentralisation to be democratic, more is implied than just a downward transfer of authority to political actors and institutions at a lower level. Johnson (2001) argues that democratic decentralisation entails a system of governance in which citizens possess the right to hold local public officials to account through the use of elections, grievance meetings, other collective action and democratic means. Barnett, Minis and Van Sant (1997) provide a conceptualisation of democratic decentralisation showing the key relationships that are defined by this term: the relationship between central government and local government, which they call decentralisation, and a reciprocal relationship between local governments and citizens, which they call democratic local governance. They argue that, in decentralisation, central government transfers administrative, financial and political power to local government institutions, whereas democratic local governance looks beyond local government administration and service delivery to focus on institutions and structures that enable people to decide and do things for themselves. Democratic local governance thus emphasises the presence of mechanisms for fair political competition, accountability and government processes that are transparent and responsive to the public. Blair (2000:21) captures the essence of this idea with the following definition of democratic decentralisation:

Meaningful authority devolved to local units of governance that are accessible and accountable to local citizenry who enjoy full political rights and liberty. It combines participation with accountability – the ability of the people to hold local government responsible for how it is affecting them.

This brief review has highlighted the difficulties in defining the term "decentralisation" as a standard notion. It appears that what is meant by decentralisation is closely related to the specific social, economic and political context. In Malawi, the history of decentralisation shows that various understandings of the term have been applied at different points in time. However, Malawi's current decentralisation reforms display a shift of emphasis from deconcentration or administrative decentralisation to devolution/political decentralisation. In particular, the current reforms are being termed "democratic decentralisation", heralded by the slogan *mphamvu ku wanthu* ("power to the people"). Thus, the current understanding of decentralisation as a means of fostering more efficient public service delivery is being explicitly linked with democratisation, accountability and enhancement of participation at community level.

Decentralisation Efforts in Malawi

Colonial period (1891-1961)

The move towards decentralisation in Malawi is part of an unfolding process that goes back to the country's history both during the colonial period and Dr Banda's single-party era. Initially, the British introduced a deconcentrated form of administration through the policy of indirect rule where judicial, administrative and development powers were devolved to chiefs under the 1933 Native Authorities Ordinance. However, the chief's political powers were reoriented and circumscribed under the strict control of the colonial administration through the district commissioners (DCs). The system changed during the late colonial period with the passage of the District Councils Ordinance of 1953 that established formal statutory local government councils separate from the native authorities. Through this legislation, local government councils were given some authority to make bylaws and provide health, education, agriculture and other services. Even though the purpose of these changes, at least from the perspective of the colonial office, was to provide for the political education of the indigenous Malawians through practice, none of the members of these bodies were elected (Kaunda 1999). Unlike the urban areas, in the rural districts where this initiative was implemented, the council members were still appointed by the DCs in conjunction with the chiefs. From the political readings of the nature of decentralisation policy reforms since the inception of the colonial regime, we can infer that, much as the reforms were linked to efforts to redress incapacities in public management, there were clear colonial tendencies towards control and centralisation. These included the recourse to chiefs rather than locally elected local government as recipients of decentralised powers under the strict control of the central government representative (the DC), the postponement of the election principle in favour of government appointment in the choice of council members, the amendment made to the 1953 act in the late 1950s that stripped councils of all rule-making powers and limited their role to that of service providers for fear that nationalists would capture the councils and further the anti-colonial struggle (Kaunda 1999). These examples reflect the colonial government's perception of local government as a potential threat to state consolidation. This illustrates an important feature of Malawi's historical legacy that has been clearly manifested in various forms under different regimes and has influenced the direction, extent and impact of contemporary decentralisation reforms, as I show later in this paper.

Decentralisation after Self-government and Independence (1961-1965)

When Malawians gained control of the central government in 1961, they demonstrated a commitment to decentralisation based on devolution of powers. In building on the system of decentralised local government established by the colonial government, the nationalist government made a number of changes. Through the Local Government (District Councils) Amendment Ordinance of 1961, the government introduced statutory district councils in all districts and provided for universal adult suffrage in the election of council members. District councils assumed all the responsibilities of the pre-independence councils. In particular, councils became local education authorities, highway authorities, and public health authorities, functions that were formerly under the control of the DCs (Apthorpe, Chiviya and Kaunda 1995). Apthorpe, Chiviya and Kaunda further note that, through these changes, the councils played an important role in providing public health facilities, building rural dispensaries and operating maternity clinics. They were also responsible for supervising markets, water supplies and slaughterhouses, as well as for building and maintaining roads, bridges and ferries in rural areas. In addition to these important functions, local government authorities also operated postal agencies and provided community centres, libraries, sports grounds, home craft centres and adult literacy classes.

Some analysts consider this period as the golden age of local government in Malawi. Council members were democratically elected, councils provided a variety of services that were valued by their communities and government supported the councils with adequate grants (Apthorpe, Chiviya and Kaunda 1995; Kutengule et al. 2004). These observations lend credence to propositions provided in the decentralisation literature (Manor 1999; Smoke 2003) about the value of a supportive public, sufficient powers to exercise influence over development activities and financial support from central government in providing crucial and helpful conditions for the success of decentralisation in improving public service delivery. This period was short-lived, however, as the following section describes.

Shifting Sands: The Dismantling of Elected Local Government and the Revival of the District Focus Policy of Decentralisation (1965-1993)

The installation of Dr Banda's one-party state in 1966 heralded a decline in the fortunes of decentralised, elected local government in Malawi. The inherent dynamics of the one-party state's need to consolidate its power led to the dismantling of elected local government, and popular participation was forcibly moulded into a role prescribed by the party (Cross and Kutengule 2001). First, the procedures for election to local government councils were altered in October 1966. The original district council election rules of 1962, which provided for democratic elections, were made subject to party selection, thus reversing the principle of elected, representative local government. Instead, within each ward, the party had to nominate at least three and not more than five candidates and then forward these names to the president, who would then select one candidate to represent the ward (Kaunda 1999). Further, all local councillors had to belong to the party and had to be ex-officio members of the area committee of the party. Any elected council member had to vacate his seat if he left the party. Beyond this, the activities of party members had further ramifications for the efficient operations of local government councils. For example, party officials stayed in local council rest houses free and used council vehicles as and when they wanted, without paying for them. They also refused to pay local government rates and fees either for party functions or for personal use, and nobody could challenge them, since the party was supreme (Apthorpe, Chiviya and Kaunda 1995).

In addition, Banda's government's orientation towards central control of all aspects of governance emphasised implementation of development functions through deconcentration of sectoral ministries from the centre to the region, district and sub-district levels. Thus, central-government offices operated side-by-side with district councils in each district. Through these trends, central government systematically began to transfer some of the functions and responsibilities of district councils to these offices. At the same time, it took over the posting of all district councils' senior staff and progressively restricted the councils' freedom to fix and collect revenue (Mbeye 1998).

Government's decision to create district development committees (DDCs) further contributed to the decline. From the mid-1960s, an important development in the decentralisation movement in Africa was the realisation that development goals in the field could not be effectively pursued in situations in which field offices and local government systems operated in isolation of one another in the development process. This need led to the creation of DDCs:

> [B]y the close of the first decade of independence District Development Committees existed in practically all Anglophone Africa and the common practice was for one country to replicate the structures in operation in a neighbouring country; often there would be a consultant from a donor country initiating such replication (Oyugi 2001:106).

This development led to the turning away from district councils as the prime instrument of decentralisation in favour of DDCs (Mawhood 1993). Thus, in 1965, District Development Committees[1] were established in rural districts of Malawi with the stated intention of providing decentralised planning of local development projects in each district through popular participation (Miller 1970). The committees were envisaged as key vehicles for effecting grassroots participation and involvement in the development process. Structurally, these committees came under the district administration system operated by the Office of the President and Cabinet. Although the architects of the DDCs initially viewed them as sounding boards through which government could be appraised of district priorities, the DDCs soon changed into vehicles for enlisting community support for government-approved programmes (Miller 1970). The government permitted the creation of informal area and village action groups at sub-district level to enlist the latent enthusiasm of villagers for productive work as needed (Government of Malawi 1969). The creation of DDCs, with a mandate similar to local government councils but placed under a central government office, marked a fundamental step in Banda's sidelining of local councils in favour of an enlarged role for central government structures in rural development processes: part of a continuing trend towards central planning and control in the delivery of public services.

During the final years of Banda's rule, decentralisation reform re-appeared in the government agenda as poverty alleviation took centre stage in international policy circles. With growing evidence that structural adjustment programmes were having adverse effects on large numbers of people, the Bretton Woods institutions were compelled to shift their position on stringent economic reforms and include poverty in the adjustment agenda (Mkandawire 2003). Conspicuously, during the late 1980s and early 1990s, bilateral and multilateral donors began to give explicit recognition to the importance of human needs and good governance (World Bank 1989, 1991). As Mawhood argues, although decentralisation did not seem to be a condition for the bank's loans up to early 1992:

> the combination of policies of liberalisation and the new emphasis that ordinary people should participate more in the design and implementation of development programmes seemed to order for the introduction of an explicit policy of structural adjustment which included a requirement for decentralisation (1993:42).

In Malawi, the process of reconsidering decentralisation in light of poverty was punctuated by a number of studies. It was initially triggered by a World Bank Assessment Report of 1987/88 that concluded that the fight to eradicate poverty in Malawi could not be won without the direct involvement of people in the development process (Mbeye 2003). Further, a joint government and United Nations situation analysis of poverty was undertaken in the early 1990s in which the question of an appropriate institutional framework for poverty alleviation arose (Government of Malawi 1993). The analysis noted that the uncoordinated approach using a plethora of activities from various ministry operations at the local level tended to confuse beneficiaries. It concluded that the DDC was not an effective institutional framework for implementing rural development initiatives. The analysis recommended a participatory process in which the government, civil society and the private sector organised themselves to explore grassroots solutions to poverty. Specifically, decentralisation was highlighted as a reform process that would address this gap, but no specific mode of decentralisation was articulated in this report. Subsequently, government explicitly adopted decentralisation as an institutional objective and strategy for the implementation of poverty alleviation efforts (Department of Local Government 2001).

Around the same time, the United Nations Development Programme (UNDP) and the United Nations Capital Development Fund (UNCDF) offered to work with the Malawi government to develop and pilot a methodology for decentralised participatory planning, and financing of district-level capital investment. These initiatives were first implemented in six districts: Nkhatabay, Mchinji, Dedza, Nsanje, Thyolo and Mangochi. Suffice to note that this was part of a global agenda involving twenty-three developing countries with the aim of generating lessons and providing a basis for replicating the best practices in the design of decentralised governance reform programmes. The major aims of the reforms were to revitalise the rural development process, make the districts the focal points for planning and implementation of projects and for district development management generally and elevate popular participation as the cornerstone of decentralisation (Government of Malawi 1996; Mbeye 1998; Ssewankambo; Chiweza and Nyondo 2004).

These developments culminated in the government's adoption of the District Focus for Rural Development decentralisation policy, an adaptation of a Kenyan model of decentralisation. The implementation of this programme relied on existing structures of the DDC system, albeit with some modifications that were done to ensure that districts assumed a leadership role in matters of local governance and development through enhanced capacity for district planning and financial autonomy (Mbeye 2003). However, the nature, scope and content of the policy were limited to administrative deconcentration of service provision and delivery responsibilities of line ministries. It did not include elected local representative institutions (Mbeye 1998). This observation offers a plausible explanation for government's positive attitude towards the reform given the regime's history of deference towards centralised rule. Nevertheless, a critical point of departure for the 1993 decentralisation reforms is that this round of policy innovation was largely a function of macro-variables that were external in origin. The reforms were not the result of an evolutionary process from below reflecting people's desire for participation in development and governance, or even the result of government's own policy analysis. This is in line with observations that have been made in other countries about decentralisation reforms in the 90s: they were all influenced by external reformist trajectories that promoted values of participation, transparency and accountability (Schoburgh 2007; Olowu 2001).

The successes of the district focus policy led to a further UNDP-supported programme called the Local Governance and Development Management Programme (LGDMP), whose aims were twofold: 1) to support further decentralisation policy development; and 2) to replicate the district planning system in all of Malawi's districts (ECIAfrica 2007). The LGDMP, implemented from 1998 to 2001, had three main components: 1) strengthening the capacity of central and local government to formulate and implement decentralisation policy, 2) strengthening the capacity of central and local government, districts and communities in planning and managing local development and service delivery and 3) instituting appropriate procedures and processes for financing local authorities in support of their decentralised service responsibilities.

Democratic Decentralisation and the Revival of Local Government Councils (1994 to 2006)

Decentralisation gained new impetus with the political changes that took place in 1994 as the new, democratically elected government sought to revamp the machinery of government. Decentralisation featured prominently in the 1994 Malawi constitution, and the language employed in this document in effect linked the agenda of decentralisation with democratisation, development and effective public management. The 1994 constitution provided for the strengthening of previously defunct local government institutions by allowing for the creation of a new wave of rural and urban local government authorities with responsibility for 'welfare provision; consolidation and promotion of local democratic institutions and participation; the promotion of infrastructure and economic development through … local development plans; and the representation to central government of local development plans' (Government of Malawi 1994: Chapter XIV). However, even though constitutional provisions provided the vision for the desired local government system, they did not provide direction on the types of institutional arrangements that should be set up for decentralisation. Cabinet therefore commissioned a review of all decentralisation efforts in the country in order to come up with a new policy that would embody the spirit of the constitution. Lessons derived from the pilot districts also fed into the decentralisation policy formulation process and the promulgation of the Local Government Act (ECIAfrica 2007).

The 1998 decentralisation policy integrates governmental agencies at the district and local levels into one administrative unit (called the assembly) through a process of institutional integration, manpower absorption, composite budgeting and provision of funds for the decentralised services. Additionally, the policy assigns functions and responsibilities to the various levels of government and promotes popular participation in the governance and development of the districts. Implicit in this reform process are changes in the structure and internal administration of local governments as well as adjustments in intergovernmental relations. Each assembly is meant to incorporate under one authority the previous district councils and all the ministry offices and departments represented at the district level. Elected councillors are supposed to exercise decision-making powers on behalf of the people while the day-to-day work of the assemblies is carried out by a group of professional appointed officials headed by a chief executive.[2]

Decentralisation is intended to promote participatory planning at sub-district level and representative democracy at the district level through the election of councillors to the district assemblies. The theory on which this was based is that democratic decentralisation leads to improved service delivery. Democratic decentralisation is also seen as a way of achieving governance in conformity with pillar four of the government's Poverty Reduction Strategy Paper (PSRP) of 2000-2005. Functionally, the policy and the 1998 Local Government Act explicitly assign assemblies to be the overall district authorities with responsibility for governance, development planning and provision of a wide range of district services including health, education, water, public amenities, environmental services, agriculture, community development and community police. The central government is required to devolve powers, functions, responsibilities and resources to enable the assemblies to perform their roles but is also expected to continue to be responsible for national projects, policy guidance and monitoring and inspection of the local government activities (Government of Malawi 1998). The expectation was that this would improve the delivery of goods and services at all levels as part of the government's poverty reduction strategy.

To translate these ideals into reality, the government adopted an incremental, phased approach to decentralisation through a ten-year national decentralisation programme divided into two phases. The first phase was for a period of four years (2000-2004) and focused on seven components: legal reforms, institutional development and capacity building, building a democratic culture, fiscal decentralisation, accounting and financial management, sector devolution and local development planning and financing mechanisms. How have these initiatives been implemented so as to enhance efficient delivery of public services and accountability of the local government system? This question is addressed in the following section by focusing on the implementation performance of some of the key areas of the reform. The data used here is largely drawn from reviews and evaluations that have been undertaken at the request of the government in conjunction with its development partners since 2001.[3]

i) Institutional reforms and capacity building
This process was initiated in 1999 when the former district administration offices of the central government, previously headed by district commissioners, were integrated with district councils to form district assemblies, at least in the rural

areas. Geographically, the local government authorities remained the same but were renamed assemblies, a change symbolising their new status and importance. By 2004, forty assemblies had been created with twenty-eight being predominantly rural and termed district assemblies. A further three were urban (one municipal and eight town assemblies).

However, despite this new local-government structure, the internal structure of the assemblies has not transformed them into an object of effective service delivery because the departments from the line ministries have not been fully integrated into the assembly secretariats. The absence of a unified management structure is a major stumbling block to integration and absorption of devolved sector functions. It is understood that the functional review of 2004 made recommendations regarding the structure of assemblies that have since been approved by government, but these recommendations have yet to be implemented by the treasury through issuance of an establishment warrant. The absence of an establishment warrant has also created a situation where there is considerable duplication and overlap in the provision of support services.

As things stand, there is no framework for properly integrating and absorbing functions devolved by the sectors to the district assembly. In the absence of a unified management structure, the current devolution is likely to create a number of practical management problems for district commissioners, especially with regard to personnel management matters, since staff belong to different service commissions. Some staff are recruited by the Local Government Service Commission (LGSCOM), including those recruited by the local authorities' appointments and disciplinary committees on behalf of LGSCOM. Other staff are recruited by respective sector commissions (education, health, etc.), while the Civil Service Commission recruits others. These multiple recruitment processes pose challenges regarding staff reporting and career progression, and call for the development of local government structures with harmonised human-resource management procedures. Complicating matters further is the absence of a unitary salary structure for assembly staff, which is leading to a loss of motivation and team spirit among assembly staff.

Decentralisation shifts the structure of local accountability from central government to local constituents, but the effectiveness of this shift depends on the strength of structures in place at local level. Currently, the local government act is silent on the administrative structures of central government as well as the legal structures below the district assemblies. Consequently, sectoral ministries are creating their own parallel structures, some of which are clearly in conflict with the spirit of decentralisation. This problem is compounded by ambiguity in the definition of the geographical planning unit at the district level. Is it the extension planning area, constituency, health delivery point or ward that is the recognised functional planning unit? This ambiguity makes it difficult for key district development processes to coordinate their development activities at various levels. The debate as to which institutional planning structure below the assembly should be officially recognised remains unresolved; the issue is whether it should ward or area development committee.

To make matters worse, the district assemblies have not been able to retain staff in key areas such as finance and administration. Consequently, significant gaps exist in the numbers and quality of personnel at assembly level. These gaps are especially acute in the Finance Directorate, given the need for accountability for the huge amounts of money being channelled through the district assemblies. Despite these gaps, the assemblies have not been able to recruit for some years, partly because of budgetary restrictions as a result of the expenditure-control mechanisms government has been employing under some adjustment programmes. At the same time, capacity-building efforts to support decentralisation have tended to favour individuals, particularly at the national level, many of whom then leave, rather than build lasting capacity. For example, an analysis of expenditures under the Malawi Decentralised Governance Programme supported by UNDP and UNCDF, who have been the key players of the national decentralisation programme, revealed that 75 per cent of total funding for the programme went to capacity building and 74 per cent of these funds went to national capacity-building programmes (ECIAfrica 2007). A key lesson here is that capacity building that focuses on national institutions can end up having very limited impact on service delivery to meet the needs of the poor at local level.

ii) Sector devolution
Sector devolution is a process of integrating all other departments and line ministry offices represented at the district level into the assembly and transferring relevant functions as a prerequisite for deepening and consolidating decentralisation. In Malawi, this process was delayed, and when it did finally happen, it was not properly managed, resulting in challenges of management control and direction by the DC over devolved staff in terms of discipline, recruitment, promotion, performance and reporting. The national decentralisation policy approved in October 1998 detailed service-delivery obligations for the central and local governments. The central government, through the line ministries, was entrusted with responsibility for overall policy formulation, guidance and enforcement, provision of guidelines and standards, quality control, efficient use of resources, inspection and technical assistance – as well as implementation of services of a national character. To implement the division of tasks for service delivery between sector ministries and local authorities, the Ministry of Local Government and Rural Development released guidelines for sector devolution in July 2001. Each sector ministry was required to prepare a detailed list of functions to be

devolved and to produce a sector devolution plan, but, by the end of 2003, nothing had yet materialised. The 2004 review of decentralisation noted that there was entrenched reluctance amongst key sectoral ministries to devolve their functions and resources to the local assemblies; yet this is what is at the centre of the whole process of decentralisation. This reluctance is attributed to fear among politicians and government officials of losing control over resources, along with lack of popular awareness and understanding of decentralisation (Kutengule et al. 2004).

In order to correct this situation, the Office of the President and the cabinet issued a circular ordering line ministries to transfer their functions by 1 January, 2004, but this move did not prove effective; only four out of the twenty-eight ministries developed guidelines for doing so. Compounding this state of affairs is poor orientation of ministry staff to the devolution process, since the Ministry of Local Government had not yet developed a comprehensive strategy to guide the devolution process. By 2007, only seven sectors had devolved their functions to the assemblies, and, even though the decentralisation policy devolves the service delivery planning, budgeting and management responsibilities of some sectors such as education, agriculture, health and environment to the district assemblies, recent assessments reveal that only limited devolution of these responsibilities has occurred (Nordic Consulting Group 2007). The assessment reveals that only the recurrent budgets are fully devolved, while sector development budgets are still centralised. It also shows that various ministries such as education, health and environment still maintain their own parallel district implementation plans developed through parallel processes geared towards meeting the sector standards and targets. This resulted in limited cross-sectoral analysis of issues in the local authorities, and opportunities for sector synergies were not maximised. In addition, sector staff are faced with dual reporting constraints to the DC (mainly for ORT issues) and the respective sector ministries for substantive matters (recruitment, inspection, promotions, discipline, etc.). Moreover, sectors still operate their own parallel administrative and service delivery structures, and, at the sub-district level, there are numerous committees that are not well-coordinated, leading to a lot of overlaps in activity implementation. Overall, therefore, sector devolution has not fully taken root, and most sectors exhibit more elements of deconcentration than devolution. This has made local development coordination more, rather than less, difficult for the district assemblies, with negative effects on service delivery.

iii) Fiscal decentralisation

Fiscal decentralisation has been pursued through the establishment of a local-government financing system, the strengthening of revenue collection by assemblies, training of accounting personnel and fiscal reforms, including the development and implementation, in a phased manner, of a system for inter-governmental transfer. The sources of local authority revenues in Malawi include locally generated revenue from property rates, ground rates, fees, licences, business-related activities and service charges; funds transferred by central government, including the General Resource Fund (GRF), ORT, sector funds and ceded revenues; resources provided by donors and NGOs; and loans and overdrafts from within Malawi.

Chart 2.1 below uses statistics from the twelve districts under the Malawi Decentralised Governance Programme to show that, six years after decentralisation started in 2000, the share of locally generated revenues within the total basket of assembly revenues is still very minimal. On the other hand, locally generated revenues are of critical importance for local accountability and ownership as well as the sustainability and viability of the entire system of decentralisation (Ssewankambo, Chiweza and Nyondo 2004). Local revenues are also usually applied to operational activities and only rarely apportioned towards development activities. As a result, the development budget is over 90 per cent donor-driven. In addition, there is no consideration of the recurrent cost implications of development activities. Various reviews of decentralisation have revealed very little evidence of maintenance of development projects being done. The problem is most severe with water projects, where more than 55 per cent of water facilities in the districts are not operational due to maintenance problems (ECIAfrica 2007).

Chart 2.1: **Overall district assembly revenues**

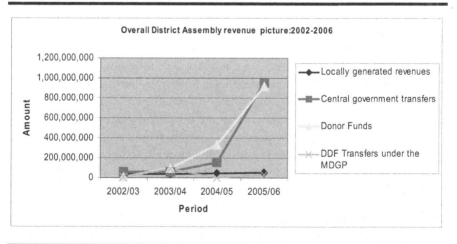

Source: ECI Africa 2007

Chart 2.1 also illustrates the rapidly growing relative share of central government and donor shares in revenues that reach the districts. Most of the government funds relate to sector transfers provided under sector-wide approaches to support deconcentrated sector development driven by the sector ministries, rather than decentralised development accountable to the assemblies. These trends significantly reduce the autonomy and downward accountability of the assemblies. With respect to donor support it is worth pointing out that initially only UNDP/ UNDCF, the Norwegian Embassy and USAID were committed to supporting the programme, but these were later joined by GTZ and ADB. However, there have been various changes in funding. UNDCF promised to contribute US$6 million, but then cut back its allocation to US$1.5 million. The Norwegian Embassy suspended its funding, citing lack of commitment by government to local democratic processes. These cutbacks had serious negative impacts in districts that were heavily supported by UNCDF and the Norwegian Embassy, where there was virtually no funding to cater for development projects and other related activities. In short, a sustainable financial base for the assemblies has not been developed, which calls into question the overall sustainability of Malawi decentralisation initiatives in promoting efficient and effective service delivery.

iv) Building a democratic culture

Activities in this component have mainly focused on civic education to raise public awareness of decentralisation. Since the adoption of the National Decentralisation Policy in 1998, and the passing of the Local Government Act, a number of initiatives have been taken in order to popularise the strategy of transferring power, responsibilities and financial resources from central to local government – and, in particular, to explain the district and sub-district structures and processes that have been established in order to plan and implement development projects in a participatory manner. However, there is still limited understanding of decentralisation and participation by the general population. Although community members do know about decentralisation – particularly through the intensive radio campaigns that have been conducted – they have generally interpreted the 'Power to the People' slogan and the concept of participation as simply the power to identify development needs and ask for assistance (Nordic Consulting Group 2007). There is certainly a lot of participation taking place in Malawian communities, but it consists mainly of contributions of sand, water and unpaid labour to development projects rather than emphasising the individual and collective agency of communities to influence and make demands for better service delivery.

This limited view of participation can be attributed to several factors: (1) the concept of participation implicit in the many donor-driven models supporting decentralisation that emphasise community contributions as a precondition for assembly support, and (2) an over-concentration of central-level and assembly-level officials in capacity-building efforts at the expense of grassroots structures. The question, then, is what sort of participation would lead to empowerment of communities beyond the blueprints provided by various donor programmes? This is an issue that deserves some reflection in Malawi.

The achievement of a democratic culture has further been constrained by the continual postponement of local elections. Since 2005, when the term of office for councillors elected in 2000 expired, there have been no elected councillors in the assemblies. The functions of the assemblies are now being performed by district consultative committees, also known as district development committees in some places. They are composed of people supposed to be ex-officio members of the assemblies (MPs, TAs, NGOs), with final decisions being made by the assembly secretariat after recourse to the centre in a number of cases. This reflects a return to the 1960s style of district development committees and has a number of troubling implications. First, it means there is limited accountability and democratisation at the local level. A key goal of public-sector reforms was to raise the accountability of local government authorities. Accountability implies a measure of "answerability" for actions taken, and an obligation for public officials and representatives to inform and explain – to enter, on equal terms, into communication with their constituents. However, in Malawi, a situation of limited accountability persists; there are few formal consultations with citizens, limited feedback to the communities and little downward accountability. The result is a lack of democratisation and a lack of formal links between the community and district staff. Yet it has been argued that political decentralisation, when accompanied by a strong legal framework, can create local accountability and thereby foster officials' legitimacy, bolstering citizen involvement and interest in politics and deepening the democratic nature of institutions (Blair 2000; Crook and Manor 1998).

Second, many of the decisions made in the local authorities are not legally binding, including the approval of plans and budgets and setting of fees to be levied by the local authorities. In addition, the local authorities cannot pass by-laws necessary to regulate operations in the local authorities. Moreover, there are limited checks and balances. The district executive committees (DECs) are now mixing the decision-making (political) and implementation (technical) functions, limiting checks and balances. This is especially the case because civil-society organisations, especially in local authorities, are not equipped to perform the "watchdog" function effectively. Practically speaking, the local authorities are performing as deconcentrated units of central government – reporting to the central government organs rather than to the respective assemblies.

v) Coordination of the reform programme

The political and economic crisis of 1994 presented a unique opportunity for reform, and a small and highly effective policy group within government, supported by some development partners, were able to sustain a momentum for change that culminated in the passing of the decentralisation policy and Local Government Act of 1999. However, because of a number of changes on the political front and within government itself, the political will and technical commitment needed to complete the preparation and successful implementation of devolution has not been sustained. This has resulted in numerous coordination problems that have stalled sector devolution. Without a solid political base of support, decentralisation cannot be successfully implemented. In this regard, the various reviews of decentralisation have highlighted the noticeable absence of a body at the national level with sufficient authority to effectively drive the process of decentralisation at either the political or technical level. Although the ministry has established a decentralisation unit to coordinate the decentralisation process countrywide, the unit lacks adequate technical capacity, as the majority of technical posts are vacant. Even when these are filled, it is not likely that staff will be able to perform their work effectively without significant further capacity building.

The Inter-Ministerial Technical Steering Committee (IMTSC) that was supposed to provide the coordination mechanism and a platform for cross-sector discussion of issues is not functional and hardly ever meets. This has affected the pace of coordination both within the sectors and between government and development partners. As a result, strategic partnerships have not been established with all the key stakeholders, including sector ministries as well as donors supporting service delivery by district assemblies. For example, while UNDP was espousing decentralisation with a district development fund, its sister institution, the World Bank, chose to implement its own Malawi Social Action Fund through independent structures. Meanwhile, the European Union continues to implement its micro-projects outside government structures. Lack of coordination has also led to different donors funding particular portions of the reform and particular districts. This has resulted in an uncoordinated implementation of development projects, fuelled funding disparities among districts and leading to varied designs and specifications being used for similar projects depending on the donor.

Similarly, some national programmes and NGOs operating at district level have tended to undermine the objectives of decentralisation by operating outside decentralised structures, a practice that poses challenges for the coordination and sustainability of the programmes. A development worth reflecting on here is the creation of the constituency fund for development projects in parliamentary constituencies. Under this initiative, the government allocates development funds quarterly to all constituencies. The funds are at the discretion of the local member of parliament. This effectively sidelines the district development fund, which is the recognised local authority development-funding structure and undermines the role of local government in local development decision-making. Likewise, the ineffectiveness of the Cabinet Committee on Decentralisation, which is responsible for providing policy guidance, has created a vacuum. There is no political champion for the implementation of the decentralisation policy and issues arising from the implementation of the decentralisation process are not being resolved, which has led to a loss of momentum. As a result, the National Decentralisation Programme II adopted by parliament in 2004 to guide the implementation of the decentralisation policy for the period 2005-2009 has still not been officially launched, let alone implemented.

The fragmented efforts towards consensus building and commitment to the devolution of functions from line ministries to assemblies in Malawi can also be traced to the weak design of the whole public sector reform programme. With no clear definition of the authorities responsible for implementation, monitoring and evaluation, ministries have tended to act autonomously. The tripartite review of the public sector reform process in Malawi that was carried out in 2005 revealed a number of weaknesses including limited government ownership, a continued absence of a dedicated central unit responsible for providing leadership and coordination of public sector reforms, a coordinating ministry that did not necessarily drive most of the activities implemented and lack of synergies and coordination with and between the implementing points. In relation to the last point, Duverall (2001) highlights the omission of decentralisation in the functional reviews as a typical problem of coordination and weak synergies between decentralisation and other reforms under the PSRP that rendered the reviews irrelevant. Yet the functional reviews that government ministries were supposed to undertake are vital; they aid definition of mission statements and organisational structures, clarify issues of responsibility and accountability and eliminate duplication of functions.

Concluding Reflections and Lessons

Even though great progress has been made in decentralisation policy formulation, local government in Malawi remains largely an extension of the central government, despite the fact that community participation has frequently been cited as the underlying principle of decentralisation. Central government is still playing a key role in service delivery, as the functions are not fully devolved to local authorities.

While the theoretical foundations of the kind of decentralisation Malawi adopted emphasised institutional reform to enhance participation of the poor in decision-making and to make public managers more responsive, the programme has largely focused on implementing a one-size-fits-all approach based on UNCDF's best practices. Thus, even though assemblies have been created as new institutions of decentralisation at the district level, the model did not entail significant transformation of previous institutional frameworks governing sub-district decentralisation. Instead, a lot of attention was given to improving the technical aspects of decentralisation such as development of systems, training manuals and implementation of development projects with an emphasis on the use of capital grants, while paying little attention to the preferences and incentives of different actors such as communities, sector ministry staff, local government staff and political actors. Inadequate attention has also been paid to the question of promoting accountability, particularly with respect to the appropriateness and characteristics of institutional structures and mechanisms that should be put forward to ensure that people are able to demand accountability from their leaders and take control of their destinies.

As Mohan and Stokke (2000) argue, decentralisation constitutes a fluid and flexible discourse that can be utilised by different ideological interests. In the Malawi case, two key interests are evident. On the one hand, donor interest in promoting decentralisation has been evident and varied, with some donors pushing for social funds and others pushing for capital development funds. On the other hand, government interest and commitment has not been stable from one political regime to the other, and the role of the president has been pivotal in influencing the direction of reforms. What is discernible throughout the various regimes is the overriding interest to employ decentralisation to further the interests of the ruling elite and to consolidate the state and enhance delivery of centrally designed programmes. This has had a direct bearing on how political championship has pushed certain reform initiatives forward. A good example is how each regime appears to dilly-dally on issues of local elections, a critical element of democratic decentralisation that provides a linkage between public service providers and the citizens. Much as public-sector reform has technical aspects, it is also a social and political phenomenon driven by human behaviour and other local circumstances. Thus, in the absence of sustained political and bureaucratic will to move forward with the reforms and improve the prospects for implementation, public-sector reforms cannot achieve their objectives simply by focusing on technocratic components such as functional reviews, installation of new systems, redesigning of organisational charts, training of staff, etc.

The Malawi experience also demonstrates the challenge of implementing programmes with a multiplicity of objectives. Decentralisation in Malawi has a number of objectives, related to development, governance and democratisation. However, the actual implementation of programmes has tended to focus on the development side, with very little emphasis on governance and democratisation. The Malawi experience also demonstrates the challenge of pursuing NPM-inspired reforms in the context of structural adjustment programmes that emphasise expenditure cuts, while governance objectives entail significant investment in institutional development and capacity building. Public-expenditure controls in areas such as recruitment have had a significant impact on the staffing situation of most local authorities in Malawi, crippling their ability to deliver services effectively.

Finally, given Malawi's history of centralised rule and administration, the kind of reform adopted was an ambitious programme for service-delivery improvement, entailing fundamental transformation in the conduct of public affairs and relations between citizens and the state. The sequencing and prioritisation of the reforms needed to focus first on getting the basics right, such as issues of staffing and capacity of the assemblies, producing a shared sector-devolution strategy, rationalising sub-district participatory structures and developing community capacities, before embarking on the actual transfer of responsibilities. Instead limited government and donor funding, the suspension of local-government elections and NDP II have, in effect, stalled the decentralisation initiative. Along with sector devolution driven by a SWAP approach, these factors have, de facto, produced deconcentration rather than devolution in Malawi. This is a continuing thread in Malawi's history, and it calls into question the prospects for democratic decentralisation reforms. Putting Malawi back onto a path of sustainable decentralisation will require not only political will and championship from the highest levels of government, but also the mobilisation of widespread donor support to re-launch the national decentralisation programme.

Notes

1. Although established in 1965, the committees only became operational in September 1966 after the first training courses were introduced for members.
2. In the rural areas the chief executive is still known as a district commissioner. Government took this decision to avoid confusing the rural masses.
3. The following major reports in order of the most recent explain these observations in detail: ECIAfrica, 2007, *Malawi: Final Evaluation of the UNDP and UNCDF's Local Development*. Final Draft Evaluation Report submitted to UNCDF/UNDP; Nordic Consulting Group, 2007, *Aligning Central Government, Local Authorities and Communities for Better Service Delivery*. Evaluation report submitted to the World Bank; Ssewankambo, Chiweza and Nyondo, 2004, *Mid Term Review of the UNDP Decentralised Governance Programme* (November/December); Phiri and Chima, 2004, *A Review of the Planning system in Line with National Planning Policies and Frameworks*; Kutengule et al., 2004, *Joint Donor/Government Review of the National Decentralisation Programme of Malawi*; Chinsinga and Dzimadzi, 2001, *An Impact Assessment on the Process of Decentralisation in Malawi*.

References

Agrawal, A. and Ribot, J., 1999, 'Accountability in Decentralisation: A Framework with South Asian and African cases', *Journal of Developing Areas*, Vol. 33, pp. 473-502.

Apthorpe, R. A., Chiviya, E. C. and Kaunda, G., 1995, *Decentralisation in Malawi: Local Governance and Development*, Lilongwe: United Nations Development Programme and Ministry of Local Government and Rural Development.

Bardhan, P., 2002, Decentralisation of Governance and Development, *Journal of Economic Perspectives,* Vol 16, No 4, pp. 185-205.

Barnett, C. C., Minis, H., and Van Sant, J., 1997, *Democratic Decentralisation,* Unpublished paper prepared for USAID by Research Triangle Institute.

Blair, H., 2000, 'Participation and Accountability at the Periphery: Democratic Local Governance in Six Countries', *World Development,* Vol. 28, No. 1, pp. 21-39.

Conyers, D., 2000, 'Decentralisation: A Conceptual Analysis (Part 1)', *Local Government Perspectives*, Vol. 7, No. 3. Pp. 7-9.

Cheema, G. and Rondinelli, D., 1983, Decentralisation and Development: Policy Implementation in Developing Countries, London: Sage.

Chinsinga, B. and Dzimadzi, C., 2001, *Impact Assessment Study on the Process of Decentralisation in Malawi since 1993*, Lilongwe: Decentralisation Secretariat.

Chiweza, A., 2005, 'Participation: Reality of Rhetoric in Rural Communities of Malawi', *Tanzanet Journal*, Vol. 15, No.1, pp. 1-8.

Crook, R. C. and Manor, J., 1998, *Democracy and Decentralisation in South Asia and West Africa,* Cambridge: Cambridge University Press.

Department of Local Government, 2001, *Development Planning Handbook for District Assemblies*, Lilongwe: Department of Local Government.

ECIAfrica, 2007, 'Malawi: Final Evaluation of the UNDP and UNCDF's Local Development', Evaluation Report submitted to UNCDF/UNDP.

Government of Malawi, 1969, *District Development Committees*, Zomba: Government Printer.

Government of Malawi, 1993, *Parliamentary and Presidential Act No. 31,* Zomba: Government Printer.

Government of Malawi, 1994, *The Republic of Malawi Constitution of 1994.* Zomba: Government Printer.

Government of Malawi, 1996, Malawi Decentralisation Policy Implementation: Capacity Assessments and Resource Needs Study, Lilongwe: Government of Malawi and UNDP.

Government of Malawi, 1998, *The Local Government Act, No. 42 of the Laws of Malawi,* Zomba: Government Press.

Government of Malawi, 2002, *Public Sector Reform Programme*, Zomba: Government Printer.

Grant, U., 2002, Local Government Decision Making: Citizen Participation and Local Government Accountability, A Literature Review, Birmingham: International Development Department, University of Birmingham.

Gurukkal, R., 2000, *Coalition of Conflicting Interests and the Politics of Decentralisation: A Theoretical Critique.* Paper presented at the International Conference on Democratic Decentralisation, Kerala, India.

Johnson, C., 2001, 'Local Democracy, Democratic Decentralisation and Rural Development: Theories: Challenges and Options for Policy', *Development Policy Review,* Vol. 19, No. 4, pp. 521-532.

Kaunda, M., 1999, 'State Centralisation and the Decline of Local Government in Malawi', *International Review of Administrative Sciences*, Vol. 65, No. 4, 579-595.

Kutengule, M., Watson, D., Kampanje, R., Chibwana, A., Chiteyeye, J., Matenje, I., 2004, *Report on Review of the National Decentralisation Programme of Malawi: 2001-2004*, Lilongwe: GOM, UNCDF, UNDP.

Litvack, J., Ahmad, J. and Bird, R., 1998, Rethinking Decentralisation in Developing Countries: A Review of Recent Experience. Washington DC: World Bank.

Mamdani, H., 1996, Citizen and Subject: Contemporary Africa and the Legacy of Late Colonialism. New Jersey: Princeton University Press.

Manor, J., 1999, The Political Economy of Democratic Decentralisation, Washington DC: World Bank.

Mayo, H. B., 1960, *An Introduction to Democratic Theory*. Oxford: Oxford University Press.

Mawhood, P., 1993, Local government in the Third World: The Experience of Decentralisation in Tropical Africa, 2nd ed., Johannesburg: Africa Institute of South Africa.

Mbeye, J., 1998, 'Decentralisation in Malawi: An Assessment of the Policy Process', *Bwalo: A Forum for Social Development*, Vol. 2, pp. 74 -92.

Mbeye, J., 2003, *Decentralisation Policies in Malawi*, Johannesburg: SURF, UNDP.

McGinn, N. and Welch, T., 1999, *Decentralisation of Education: Why, When, What and How?* Paris: UNESCO/International Institute for Educational Planning.

Mhone, G., 2003, 'Challenges for Governance, Public Sector Reform and Public Administration in Africa', *Paper presented at a workshop on Building an African Governance and Public Administration Support and Research Agenda*, Johannesburg, 17 February.

Miller, R., 1970, 'District Development Committees in Malawi: A Case Study in Rural Development', *Journal of Administration Overseas,* Vol. 9, No. 2, pp. 129-142.

Mkandawire, T., and Soludo C.C., 1999, *Our Continent Our Future: African Perspectives on Structural Adjustment,* Trenton: Africa World Press

Mkandawire, T., 2003, 'Freedom and Empowerment: Challenges to Democracy in Africa', in B. Immink, S. Lembani, M. Ott and C. Peters-Berries, eds., *From Freedom to Empowerment: Ten Years of Democratisation in Malawi*. Lilongwe: Forum for Dialogue and Peace, Konrad Adenauer Foundation, Malawi German Programme for Democracy and Decentralisation, National Initiative for Civic Education, pp. 13 -36.

Mohan, G. and Stokke, K., 2000, 'Participatory Development and Empowerment: The Dangers of Localism', *Third World Quarterly,* Vol. 21, No. 2, pp. 247-268.

Mukwena, M.R. and Lolojih, P.K., 2002, 'Governance and Local Government Reforms in Zambia's Third Republic', in D. Olowu and S. Saka, eds., *Better Governance and Public Policy: Capacity Building and Democratic Renewal in Africa*, Bloomfield, CT: Kumarian Press, pp. 215-230.

Nordic Consulting Group, 2007, 'Aligning Central Government, Local Authorities and Communities for Service Delivery in Malawi', Evaluation Report submitted to the World Bank.

Oakely, P., 1991, Projects with People: The Practice of Participation in Rural Development, Geneva: ILO.

Olowu, D., 2001, *Decentralisation Policies under Structural Adjustment and Democratisation in Africa*, Geneva: UNRISD.

Oyugi, W.O., 2000, 'Decentralisation for Good Governance and Development: The Unending Debate'. *Regional Development Dialogue,* Vol. 21, No. 1, pp. iii -xix.

Oyugi, W.O., 2001, 'Decentralisation in Africa', in J.S.E. Walter, B. Stohr, and D. Mani, eds., *Decentralisation, Governance and Planning for Local Level Development*, Vol. 3, Westport: United Nations Centre for Regional Development, pp. 95-122.

Ribot, J., 2002, African Decentralisation: Local Actors, Powers and Accountability, Geneva: UNRISD.

Rondinelli, D., McCullough, J.S. and Johnson, R.W., 1989, 'Analysing Decentralisation Policies in Developing Countries: A Political Economy Framework', *Development and Change*, Vol. 20, No. 1, pp. 57-87.

Rose, P., 2003, 'Community Participation in School Policy and Planning in Malawi: Balancing Local Knowledge, National Policies and International Agency Priorities', *Compare*, Vol. 33, No. 1, pp. 47-64.

Schoburgh, E.D., 2007, 'Local Government Reform in Jamaica and Trinidad: A Policy Dilemma', *Public Administration and Development*, Vol. 27, pp. 159-174.

Ssewankambo, E., Chiweza, A., and Nyondo, J., 2004, *Malawi Decentralised Governance Programme: Midterm review final report*, Lilongwe: UNDP/UNCDF.

Siddiquee, N.A., 2006, 'Public Management Reform in Malaysia: Recent Initiatives and Experiences', *International Journal of Public Sector Management*, Vol. 19, No. 4, pp. 339-358.

Slater, D., 1989, 'Territorial Power and the Peripheral State: The Issue of Decentralisation', *Development and Change*, Vol. 20, No. 3, pp. 501-531.

Smoke, P., 2003, 'Decentralisation in Africa: Goals, Dimensions, Myths and Challenges', *Public Administration and Development*, Vol. 23, No. 1, pp.7-16.

Stohr, W.B., 2001, 'Subsidiarity: A Key Concept for Regional Development Policy', in New Regional Development Paradigms, UNCRD, p. 3.

Therkildsen, O., 2001, *Efficiency, Accountability and Implementation: Public Sector Reform in East and Southern Africa*, UNRISD Paper No 3, Geneva: Programme on Democracy, Governance and Human Rights, UNRISD.

Tordoff, W., and Young, R.A, 1994, 'Decentralisation and Public Sector Reform in Zambia', *Journal of Southern African Studies*, Vol. 20, No.2, pp. 285-289.

United Nations Capital Development Fund, 2000, *Report on World Summit for Social Development*, Copenhagen: United Nations.

Work, R., 2002, *Overview of Decentralisation Worldwide: A Stepping Stone to Improved Governance and Human Development*, Paper presented at the Federalism: the Future of Decentralising States conference, Manila.

World Bank, 1983, *World Development Report*, Washington DC: World Bank.

World Bank, 1989, Sub-Saharan Africa: From Crisis to Sustainable Growth. Washington, D.C: World Bank.

World Bank, 1991, Women and Development in Malawi: Constraints and Actions, Washington DC: World Bank.

3

Public-private Partnership in the Malawian Local Assemblies: A Failed Reform Package?

Happy M. Kayuni

Introduction

One of the key areas of public-sector reform in Malawi has been the decentralisation of local assemblies. On paper, the government of Malawi places a significant value on the role of the local assemblies, and the Constitution, Act No. 7 of 1995 clearly stipulates the creation of decentralised local assembly authorities (Government of Malawi 1995). It is not surprising, therefore, that the decentralisation of government activities through local assemblies has had considerable interest from several stakeholders. Mbeye (1998:88) observes that 'decentralisation activities have indications of a growing major public management reform programme with ramifications for all other public sector and governance reforms'. PPPs have been one of the key components of this reform package.

The term "public-private partnership" refers to a contractual agreement formed between a public institution and private-sector entity to allow for greater private-sector participation in the delivery of public services. The decentralisation framework assumes that the delivery of services will hinge upon successful partnerships; hence, PPPs take central stage in the reform packages. This paper aims at assessing the viability of PPPs in local assemblies of Malawi. It begins by briefly describing Malawi's decentralised structures and follows with an analysis of the concept of PPP as well as of the conditions necessary for the successful implementation of such partnerships. The remainder of the paper discusses the challenges towards PPP implementation in Malawi's local assemblies.

The Concept of PPP

The rationale for public sector reforms is to "attempt to raise the quality of public services delivered to citizens and enhance ... capacity [in the public sector] to carry out core Government functions" (Tambulasi and Kayuni 2007a:336). There are various forms of public sector reform which include, but are not limited to, privatisation, deregulation, contracting out, downsizing and rationalisation. All fall under the realm of new public management (NPM), a managerial approach that emerged in the 1980s and 1990s to address inadequacies in the traditional model of public-sector administration (Hughes 1998:52). NPM is intended to offer a more realistic approach to public-sector management. It is sometimes described as "managerialism" or "market-based public administration" (Hughes 1998:52). The implementation of NPM-related reforms in Malawi has been at partial but incremental process.

PPP usually falls under the NPM category of contracting out. The rationale for PPPs is that "the role of the Local government [or Government proper] is not to do everything but to make sure that everything is done", which implies that "it is not government's obligation to provide services but to see to it that they are delivered" (Fourie 2000:156). The term "private sector" in PPP theory refers to 'not only ... multinational and major companies but also ... small businesses, local entrepreneurs, non-governmental organisations (NGOs), community-based organisations (CBOs), and other civic bodies' (Fourie 2000:157).

Conditions for a Successful PPP

According to Hlahla (2000:165-166), there are six requirements for a successful public-private partnership: predictability in the legal and regulatory environment, open and competitive procurement processes, well-researched and prepared transactions, government commitment, stakeholder support and a mature financial sector.

Predictability in the legal and regulatory environment entails that 'private sector partners need to know up-front what their risks are', since 'clarity of policy and regulations avoids lengthy and intense negotiation, especially with regard to financial closure' (Hlahla 2000:165). The assumption here is that government and the private sector 'have very different perceptions and approaches' and predictability in the legal and regulatory environment ensures that they 'speak the same language' (Hlahla 2000:165). Legislation can either promote or curb good financial management practices and outcomes in PPP (Burger and Ducharme 2004:21).

Open and competitive procurement processes are important because they 'exert considerable pressure on the private sector to provide effective services at reasonable costs' (Fourie 2000:163). Indeed, an open and competitive procurement process is 'the only way local government can ensure fairness in selecting the best outcome for the consumers' (Hlahla 2000:166). Similarly, well-researched and well-prepared transactions are necessary for an effective partnership contract. According to Fourie (2000:161), 'the contract is the key mechanism to manage an effective PPP [because] the form and application of the PPP contract are key determinants of the quality and efficiencies eventually achieved'. This is why it is important for assemblies to "undertake thorough feasibility studies before entering into any partnership (Fourie 2000:161). Hlahla (2000:166) makes the important observation that 'clear project data determine the outcome of the bidding process and therefore the contract itself'; more specifically, 'if information is not clear, it becomes difficult to be transparent and therefore to be fair' (Hlahla 2000:166).

Taking into consideration that PPPs are not only complex but 'often very political in nature' (Hlahla 2000:166), it is also important that the public sector provides leadership and publicly promotes private provision of infrastructure and commits to effective management of such partnerships (Hlahla 2000:166). Another way for the government to show commitment is to ensure that enabling policies are promoted as well as articulated. Similarly, stakeholder support is vital because reforms tend to create opposition. Some sectors of society inevitably lose out in the reform process, so it is important that, before a PPP is fully launched, all the key stakeholders (including the beneficiaries or target communities) are consulted in order to minimize risks for the private sector partners. In particular, private sector partners need to 'know whether any sector of the community is opposed to the project, and whether such opposition can bring the project to a halt' (Hlahla 2000:167).

Finally, a mature and stable financial sector is equally vital for the success of the PPP approach. Most private-sector institutions involved in PPP are heavily dependent on loans offered by the financial institutions. This means that a weak or inefficient financial sector can seriously hamper the growth and development of PPPs. This is even more applicable to small and medium enterprises, which have not yet been fully established in the market.

Malawi Public sector Reform and PPPs

PPPs in Malawi can be traced back to the public-sector reforms that have been implemented in phases since 1994. According to Malawi Public Sector Management (PSM):

> The major driving factors of the public reform initiatives have ... been the need to improve efficiency and effectiveness as regards the services delivered to the public and to create an enabling environment for the implementation of the core functions of the public sector and engaging the active partnership of civil society and private sector (Kamanga 2002:4).

It is quite clear, therefore, that PPPs form a critical component of the public-sector reform package. Specifically, one of the objectives of PSM emphasises the 'critical role of partnership in addressing capacity problems' (Kamanga 2002:4). The newly launched Malawi Growth and Development Strategy (MGDS) is the major government development policy document applicable for the five-year period from the 2006/07 to the 2010/2011 fiscal years. The purpose of the MGDS is 'to serve as a single reference document for policy makers in Government, the Private Sector, Non Governmental Organisations and Cooperating Partners on Government's socio-economic growth and development priorities' (Government of Malawi 1996). The MGDS acknowledges that the 'Malawi public sector has been characterised by poor management that has generated inefficiencies in the delivery of public goods and services' but notes that 'government and its development partners are already addressing some of the challenges in the sector' through various public-sector reforms (Government of Malawi 2006:18). The MGDS also recognises the role of the private sector, stating that 'private sector development and participation is a key factor in achieving sustainable economic growth' (Government of Malawi 2006:20). Through the MGDS, the government shows its specific commitment to enhancing the role of the private sector through PPPs:

> [T]he private sector will be expected to take up opportunities from the key priority activities in the MGDS. The scope of the private sector will be widened to involve them in the provision of other public goods and services through public-private sector partnerships (Government of Malawi 2006:106).

Decentralised Local Government Structures in Malawi[1]

An 'understanding of decentralisation requires explaining why it occurs, why it takes the particular forms it does, and the relation between those forms and the outcomes they produce' (Ribot 2002:7). Conyers (in Ribot 2002:8) gives four 'broad categories' of decentralisation objectives: local empowerment (or local participation), administrative efficiency and effectiveness, national cohesion and central control. These are also some of the reasons for the creation of decentralised local-government structures in Malawi, as highlighted in the Local Government Act of 1998. The act states that the Malawi decentralisation policy objectives are as follows (Government of Malawi 1998):

- to create a democratic environment and institutions in Malawi for governance and development at the local level that will facilitate the participation of the people at the grassroots level in decision making;
- to promote accountability and good governance at the local level in order to help the government reduce poverty;
- to establish strong local institutions that embrace participatory democracy;

- to strengthen and deepen democracy by bringing services and decision making closer to the public, and to improve governance by achieving accountability and transparency.

The actual implementation of decentralisation in Malawi is intended to take place in two main phases over a ten-year period, with the first phase covering the years 2000 to 2004. This first phase focused on the following components: legal reforms, institutional development and capacity building, building a democratic culture, fiscal decentralisation, accounting and financial management, sector devolution and local-development planning and financing mechanisms. Unfortunately, due to lack of funds and related problems, the second phase was not launched immediately after the first phase as planned. The second phase is currently being worked out and is at an advanced stage of planning.

Challenges of PPP Implementation in Malawi's Local Assemblies

The implementation of PPP programmes in Malawi's local assemblies has not been smooth. In the first place, the whole idea of PPP, despite having international appeal, has not been clearly articulated in the Malawi's decentralisation programme. For example, discussions on NGOs and civil-society organisations within local government circles have mainly focused on coordinating NGO activities and making sure that NGOs operate through the assemblies rather than on how to create synergies with the private sector for improved service delivery. As a result, representation of the private sector in assembly committees remains very poor. Despite the popular rhetoric of the private sector being the engine of growth, the local authorities and private sector have not developed a clear framework of understanding on how they can operate as partners in the delivery of services. This section discusses these challenges in greater detail. Specifically, it focuses on circumvention of the decentralised planning framework, incoherent partnerships among government institutions at local level, the perception of assemblies as risky partners, inadequate supervision of partners' programmes and, finally, political interference and corruption.

Circumvention of the Decentralised Planning Framework

According to the set procedures, 'any stakeholder in grassroots development is required to operate within the ambit of the decentralised planning framework, clearly stipulating its objectives, plans and operating procedures' (Chinsinga 2005:530-531). However, as Chinsinga (2005:531) observes, 'the tendency of most stakeholders, especially non-governmental organisations (NGOs) and donors … is to circumvent the decentralised planning framework altogether, claiming that it does not have the requisite capacity to deliver'. The result is that these stakeholders or NGOs are virtually unknown at the district assembly. Their 'motive for shunning the decentralised planning framework is that they view each other and the District Assemblies not as partners but as competitors in grassroots development' (Chinsinga 2005:531). This competition is intensified when 'NGOs make use of financial inducement to target either communities or government extension workers' (Chinsinga 2005:531). The end scenario is that government extension workers neglect some core public duties and concentrate on NGO activities under the guise of partnership. In addition, certain areas tend to have a higher concentration of NGOs, while other areas have few or none at all, as is the case in certain areas of Zomba district.[2] Duplication of services is inevitable in the highly concentrated areas, but, since most of the NGOs are not known at the district assembly, it is very difficult to coordinate and implement the decentralised planning framework. In fact, NGOs implement their interventions in areas where there is a high likelihood of their projects succeeding and not necessarily on the basis of the needs of the areas.

Incoherent Partnerships among Government Institutions at Local Level

According to the Director of Planning and Development (DP&D) at Zomba District Assembly, 'the decentralised structure is sometimes confusing to all of us.'[3] The organogram provides for several directorates – the District Health Officer (DHO), District Education Manager (DEM), District Agricultural Development Officer (DADO), etc. -- that are supposed to report to the district commissioner, yet all these directors, including the district commissioner, are at the same rank (P5). The end result is that directors feel more comfortable reporting directly to their ministries rather than to the district commissioner. As a result, it is very difficult for PPPs to materialize fully, because there is no sense of partnership within the public-sector organisations themselves. More importantly, there is heightened uncertainty of what specifically has to be accomplished. Although Hussein (2004:121) observes that 'currently there is no legal framework covering sector devolution plans', the reality is that the Local Government Act clearly stipulates which sectors and functions should devolve, but this has not been followed. There is a lot of resistance to change, and this has led to a situation where 'no meaningful devolution has taken place as envisaged by the Local Government Act of 1998 and the Malawi Decentralisation Policy'. Assemblies need to define 'rules for cooperation among stakeholders at various levels of society', but this can only be done 'if there [is] ... coordination and partnership among the stakeholders and a shared commitment to making the decentralised planning framework work' (Chinsinga 2005:531).

Perception that Assemblies Are Risky Partners

As Mbeye argues (1998:87), local authorities 'require powers and both financial and administrative resources to implement local decisions, projects and programmes'. However, the reality is that 'the development planning system and organisational structure is highly bureaucratic and characterised by stringent controls and delays in project funding, communication and feedback problems to local structures' (Hussein 2004:121). Such an environment is not conducive for a successful PPP, as implementation often requires substantial financial resources, especially in the initial stages. Chiweza (1998:104) observes correctly that there is 'a mistaken belief that decentralisation is a way of saving money when in fact it requires very considerable extra resources to set up properly'.

The National Local Government Finance Committee, which is provided for in section 149 of the Malawi constitution, oversees the financing of local governments. It is government policy to ensure that five per cent of net national revenue should be transferred to district assemblies as unconditional grants and that twenty-five per cent of this amount be committed to development activities (Chilungo, cited in Hussein 2004:127-8). Despite these provisions, 'most district assemblies are characterised by chronic financial problems' that, according to Kaluwa et al. (cited in Hussein 2004:128) 'is due to, among others, the narrow resource base for locally generated revenue, lengthy budgetary processes, legislative financial controls, lack of effective accounting systems, and inability to access loans'.

Currently, property tax is a major source from which the urban local authorities get their income; it is estimated that sixty to eighty per cent of local revenue is derived from the property tax on the assessed value (considered to be the market value) of properties owned by households and enterprises (Ismail et al. 1997:89). The valuation and rating law provides that assessable property includes land and all improvements situated on that land. Although property tax has great potential as a local revenue source, it has several administrative constraints that relate to poor or outdated information bases and collection problems. In the major urban centres, the process of assessment is inefficient, infrequent and often overdue.[4] For instance, although it is a legal requirement that valuations must be done every five years, most property remains under-taxed (Mwadiwa et. al., 2004:41).

Due to problems of debt collection the Zomba assembly in 2006 contracted out this responsibility to a private-sector institution, Credit Data.[5] According to the agreement, Credit Data was allocated 10 per cent of all its collections. When the contract was signed in October 2006, the total debt was K25,750,000, but by July 2007 this had gone up to K 32,088,000. Although some of the increment was due to interest charged on overdue amounts, it is clear that the private institution was not doing an effective job. However, the root of the problem is that Credit Data inherited serious administrative problems related to valuation of property. There are numerous pending court cases by property owners challenging these debts, a situation that has frustrated Credit Data made other potential private-sector partners view working with assemblies as too risky.

Inadequate Supervision of Partners' Programmes

Unlike NGOs, which are registered through the registrar general and the Council for Non-Governmental Organisations of Malawi (CONGOMA), CBOs register at the district welfare office. Before October 2006, a CBO could be registered with any government department concerned with the issues that the CBO focused on. For example, all CBOs dealing with HIV were registered at the district health office, while those dealing with orphans were registered at the district welfare office. However, due to poor coordination of government ministries at local level, it was discovered that one CBO could be registered with several government departments. Some CBOs did this in order to maximise donor funding by claiming that they were involved with the youth, orphans, HIV-positive people, etc. and seeking funding from a variety of donors. Since there were several places for registration of CBOs (before October 2006), the present scenario is that there are numerous CBOs that have identical names.

According to the district community services officer for Zomba, it is difficult to supervise CBOs 'in this complex and confusing situation'.[6] Due to inadequacy of financial resources, most assemblies are unwilling to release funds solely for monitoring of projects handled by the private sector. The assemblies mainly rely on DEC reports, which may not be accurate at all. This situation is contrary to the envisaged scenario in the MGDS, which states that 'Government will focus on public-private partnerships not only for the provision of infrastructure, but also for continuous monitoring of the private sector environment to determine solutions that will work for the benefit of Malawi' (Government of Malawi 2006:53). According to Fourie (2000:162), 'the local authority always retains its legislative responsibility regarding the delivery of services to the community'. For this reason, Fourie adds that 'the responsibility remains, even if a delivery agent other than itself is contracted to deliver the service'. Regardless of who delivers the service, supervision is still crucial, and the local authority must be able to 'demand regular information on progress and contract compliance' (Fourie 2000:162).

Political Interference and Corruption

Corruption stems directly from lack of accountability and transparency. Burger and Ducharme (2004:11) point out that accountability entails 'personal obligation' on the part of public office bearers in the sense that they are supposed to give a public account of their activities. Tambulasi and Kayuni (2007b:167) note 'personal interests, partisan politics, corruption and nepotism among others, are the main reasons for observed low accountability and transparency' and that 'more often than not, decentralisation fails to meet its promises of increased accountability and transparency'. As a result, corruption has seriously affected assemblies and resulted in poor financial management, low-quality infrastructure and loss of donor and citizen trust. A corrupt environment negatively affects PPPs, but 'a transparent process creates a better understanding of the benefits of the partnership for all' (Fourie 2000:162).

At the same time, several NGOs claimed that activities have been hampered by politicians, especially members of parliament. Some politicians have even issued commands they expect NGOs to adhere to (Kayuni 2005:47). According to the Malawi Public Procurement Act, tender proposals are supposed to be advertised through the public media, and an internal procurement committee composed of directors of various departments are then supposed to award the tender to the best competitor. However, in many cases, influential politicians put pressure on the committee to awards tenders to unsuitable applicants[7]. On the other hand, it is widely acknowledged that only an "open, transparent and competitive processes [will] ensure credibility of procurement processes ... [and] accountability to all key stakeholders" (Hlahla 2000:165).

Status of the Malawi Private Sector[8]

Given their financial constraints, local assemblies cannot viably be engaged with large private-sector organisations. Consequently, most assemblies rely on small-scale business organisations as partners. Studies show that to deliver effectively and efficiently, especially when awarded large contracts, the small-business sector has to rely heavily on loans provided by a strong financial sector. However, according to the World Bank Institute for Finance and Private Sector Development (WBIFP) (2005), the Malawi finance sector cannot adequately support small and medium enterprises (SMEs) due to 'high default rates, lack of information on trade finance products and lack of managerial expertise and track record by SMEs' (WBIFP 2005:51). Moreover, 'the participation of private investors in the economy has also remained limited due to the dominance of largely a few private sector companies, poor investor confidence, and the small size of the domestic market' (WBIFP 2005:51). The Malawi National Gemini MSE Baseline Survey 2000 found that, despite 'increasing recognition of the potential role this sector can play in Malawi's economy and especially in the livelihoods of the relatively poor', Malawi's Medium and Small Enterprise sector 'remains small compared to other countries in the region'. More importantly, the report adds that 'the country still lacks a national strategy and policy that can push the sector significantly forward' (DFID 2001:1) Little has changed for SMEs since this report:

The vast majority of Malawian businesses are unable to access finance for investment. The financial sector is "constrained ..., [and] this is especially true for smaller business enterprises which have difficulties accessing financing" and are unable to use assets (such as land) for collateral due to the present inadequate land rights and management (Government of Malawi 2006:52).

Against this background, it is extremely difficult for local assemblies to partner effectively with the private sector.

Conclusion

This paper has noted that the Malawi local assemblies are not fully prepared to efficiently and effectively embark on PPPs. The key components required for a successful partnership –predictability in the legal and regulatory environment, open and competitive procurement processes, well-researched and prepared transactions, government commitment, a mature financial sector and stakeholder support – are broadly lacking. Some of the specific challenges that need attention include circumvention of the decentralised planning framework, incoherent partnerships among government institutions at local level, a poor financial base for local government, inadequate supervision, political interference and, finally, corruption. PPPs are vital for sustainable local development, but the current framework of local assemblies in Malawi cannot support viable partnerships either with NGOs and CBOs or with small business. It is crucial that the local governance framework be revitalized and the problems highlighted above be addressed before embarking on any meaningful PPP activities. In other words, PPP at local level is a good idea whose appropriate time has not yet come.

Notes

1. It is not the purpose of this paper to give a detailed analysis of the development and process of decentralization in Malawi. See chapter two for a detailed discussion of these.
2. Interview with the Director of Planning and Development, Zomba District Assembly, 2 August 2007.
3. Interview with the Director of Planning and Development, Zomba District Assembly, 2 August 2007.
4. Major urban centres are Blantyre, Lilongwe and Mzuzu cities, Zomba municipality and Karonga, Kasungu, Salima, Dedza, Balaka, Liwonde and Lunchenza towns.
5. Interview with the Director of Finance, Zomba Municipality, 2 August 2007.
6. Interview with the District Community Services Officer for Zomba, 2 August 2007.
7. Interview with the Director of Finance, Zomba Municipality, 2 August 2007.
8. For the purposes of this section, the word "private sector" means the "business sector".

References

Burger, J. and Ducharme, G., 2004, *Financial Management and Cost Accounting for Public Service Delivery and Development*. Bellville: School of Public Management and Planning, Stellenbosch University.

Chinsinga, B., 2005, 'District Assemblies in a Fix: The perils of the Politics of Capacity in the Political and Administrative Reforms in Malawi', *Development Southern Africa*, Vol. 22, No. 4, pp. 529-548.

Chiweza, A., 1998, 'Is the Center Willing to Share Power? The Role of Local Government in a Democracy', *Bwalo,* Issue 2, pp. 93-107.

DFID, 2001, *Malawi National Gemini MSE Baseline Survey 2000*, Lilongwe: DFID.

Fourie, A., 2000, 'Public-Private Partnership at Local Governance Level: Implications for Governance and Accountability' in F. Theron, A. Rooyen and J. Baalen, J., eds., *Good Governance for People: Policy and Management*, Stellenbosch: School of Public Management and Planning.

Government of Malawi, 1995. *The constitution of the Republic of Malawi*, Zomba: Government Printer.

Government of Malawi, 1998, *The Local Government Act*, Zomba: Government Printer.

Government of Malawi, 2006, Malawi Growth and Development Strategy, Zomba: Government Printer.

Hughes, O.,1998, *Public Management and Administration: An Introduction*, London: Palgrave.

Hussein, M., 2004, 'Decentralisation and Development: The Malawian Experience', *Africa Development*, Vol. 29, No. 2, pp 106-133.

Kamanga, R., 2002, *Report on Inventory of Public Sector Reform Initiatives*. Lilongwe: Institutional Development and Management Consultant.

Kayuni, H., 2005, *The Role of Party Politics in Local Participation and Representation: Challenges and Prospects in Malawi's Local Assemblies*, Unpublished MPA thesis, University of Stellenbosch.

Mbeye, J., 1998, 'Decentralisation in Malawi: An Assessment of the Policy Process' *Bwalo,* Issue 2, pp. 74-92.

Mwadiwa, R.P., Hiwa, G.L., Banda, J., Kalimba, S., Masiya, E., Simwaka, C., 2004, *Report on the Local Government Act (1998), The National Decentralisation Policy, and Other Relevant Legislation and Policies Impacting on Local Governance*, Lilongwe: Decentralisation Secretariat.

Ribot, J., 2002, *African Decentralisation: Local Actors, Powers and Accountability*, Geneva: UNRISD.

Tambulasi R. and Kayuni, H., 2007a, 'Public Sector Reform in Malawi', in N. Patel and R. Lasvasen R., eds., *Government and Politics in Malawi*, Montfort Press, Blantyre.

Tambulasi, R. and Kayuni, H., 2007b. 'Decentralisation Opening a New Window for Corruption: An Accountability Assessment of Malawi's Five Years of Democratic Local Governance System', *Journal of Asian and African Studies*, Vol. 42, No. 2, pp. 163-183.

World Bank Institute for Finance and Private Sector Development (WBIFP), 2005, *Policy Dialogue on Trade Finance in Malawi Policy Dialog on Trade Finance in Malawi Assessment of Constraints to Investment/Trade in Malawi*, Washington: World Bank.

4

No Key Opens Every Door:
The Failure of NPM-Based Performance
Contracting in Malawi

Richard I. C. Tambulasi

Introduction

NPM has enjoyed massive publicity as a reform model in the past decade. The key to NPM is the implementation of market-based principles and policies in the management of the public sector. The aim is to enhance efficiency and effectiveness in public-service delivery. Central to the NPM management model is the employment of public servants based on performance-contract schemes. However, the problem with NPM reforms is that they assume universality. The thinking is that the NPM reforms can rectify all public-sector problems regardless of country-specific conditions. NPM is thought to be a magic key that will fit any door, and developed, developing and transitional countries have all implemented the reforms based on this belief.

Malawi was no exception. The country begun implementing contract-based performance management in 2000. The expectation was that this would herald a new chapter in the delivery of public services. However, the reforms encountered such massive challenges that the government abandoned the system in 2007 and resumed the traditional long-tenure and pensionable system. This paper examines the challenges that the NPM-based performance contract scheme encountered in Malawi and shows why these challenges forced the scheme to be abandoned.

The New Public Management

The NPM paradigm has been the preferred public-sector reform model in many countries for the past decade. Central to NPM is the implementation of market-based principles in the running of the public sector. The rationale is that, since the private sector is efficient and effective due to effective management practices, the same market principles should be applied to make the public sector efficient and effective. The underlying argument is that all organisations, whether public or private, 'need to be efficient, effective and to provide value for money' (Turner and Hulme 1997:106). Although there are varying accounts in the literature of exactly what NPM consists of, its basic components are well understood. Christopher Hood (1991:5) summarises the seven 'doctrinal' components of NPM as follows:

- Hands-on professional management in the public sector. This means 'active visible, discretionary' control of organisations from named persons at the top who are 'free to manage';
- Explicit standards of performance measurement. Here Hood means that there should be a 'definition of goals, targets, indicators of success, preferably expressed in quantitative terms, especially for professional services';
- Greater emphasis on output controls. This means that both resource allocation and rewards must be linked to performance;
- Shift to disaggregation of units in the public sector. This entails decentralisation and emphasises the 'breaking up of monolithic' public-sector organisations into small, manageable units;
- Shift to greater competition in the public sector. This means a move to 'term contracts and public tendering procedures'. In terms of recruitment, it entails contract-based employment with agreed performance standards;
- Private-sector styles of management in the public service. This means moving away from a 'military style public service ethic' and 'greater flexibility in hiring and rewards';
- Stress on greater discipline and parsimony in resource use. The emphasis here is on 'doing more with fewer resources'. It implies cutting direct costs, raising labour discipline, resisting union demands and limiting compliance costs.

Performance Contracting in NPM

The NPM model strongly champions performance-based contract employment for public managers. Turner and Hulme (1997:116) argue that the 'performance contract highlights the central issue in the reform of public sector management, that is, how to increase the responsibilities of public managers'. This is based on the slogan 'letting managers manage" (Hood 1991). According to the Economic Commission for Africa (2003:20), performance contracts specify 'standards of performance or quantifiable targets which a government requires public officials or managers of public agencies or ministers to meet over a stated period of time'. This is emphasised by Shirley and Nellis (1991:21, cited in Turner and Hulme 1997:189), who argue that performance contracting aims at 'giving management greater autonomy over the operation of the public sector and holding managers accountable by negotiating targets, monitoring and evaluating results, and rewarding managers and staff on the basis of performance'. The understanding is that 'if managers are given greater freedom to manage, they must correspondingly be under an obligation of accountability for their performance' (Minogue 1998:26). The aim is to replace 'rules-based, process-driven' public administration by 'results- oriented' public management (Osborne and Gaebler 1992). The logic is that, if managers are to assume such responsibilities, they must be both professional and entrepreneurial. They need to be dynamic, resourceful, and adaptable in managing growth and diversification, and they need to be able to use various techniques of professional management in their routine operations (Khandwala 1989:7, cited in Turner and Hulme 1997:116).

NPM in the Malawian Public Sector

The implementation of NPM reforms in Malawi did not come explicitly. They arrived instead under the banners of the Action Plan for Civil Service of 1996 and the Public Sector Management Reform Programme of 2002 (Tambulasi 2007). These programmes were heralded as efforts to 'reshape and revitalise the public service' (Government of Malawi 2002:5) and to 'introduce the most optimal organisational, institutional and individual competence' for efficient service delivery (Government of Malawi 2002:9). The understanding was that the reforms would lead to an 'entrepreneurial public service' (Government of Malawi 2002:9) that would result in the 'delivery of quality public services' (Government of Malawi 2002:5) as well as 'ensure the civil service's affordability and sustainability over time' (Government of Malawi 1996:2).

According to the Malawi government (2002:9), the reforms were to be oriented towards:

- empowering citizens;
- focusing on outcomes, not on inputs;
- being driven by mission, not rules and regulations;
- earning more, not just spending more;
- favouring market mechanisms over bureaucratic mechanisms;
- focusing on catalysing sectors, not just providing services.

The actual reforms implemented in order to realise these goals included decentralisation, downsizing, rationalisation, privatisation, user fees and cost recovery, salary structure reforms, private-public partnerships, capacity building, better public expenditure management, increased use of digital technology and a shift to performance contracting. In the following sections of this paper, we will take a closer look at the performance-contracting reforms.

Performance Contracting in the Malawian Public Sector

Malawi began implementing performance contracting in 2000 according to guidelines set out in the *Performance Management Hand Book for the Malawi Civil Service* of 2000. The system encouraged the employment of public sector managers on three-year contracts renewable upon successful achievement of performance targets. However, this was not compulsory and was only availableto managers in the grades S4/P4 (deputy directors) and above. Managers in these grades who had reservations about the new contract scheme had the option of remaining in the traditional pensionable scheme. However, the contract employment scheme included 'monetized benefits, leading to a tripling of base salaries' (Fozzard and Simwaka 2002:13). Three-quarters of eligible staff opted for contracts.

Although Durevall and Erlandsson (2005:15) note that the contract scheme was championed by the World Bank 'in an attempt to remedy some weaknesses of the pay structure', the system was touted as 'herald[ing] a new chapter in the delivery of high quality services to the public' (Government of Malawi, 2000) and offering 'better value for money by making managers focus more competently and efficiently on core functions and policy priorities of government' (Government of Malawi 1996:14). Performance contracting was therefore oriented to the achievement of a 'specific result or outcome the employee is expected to create or contribute' (Government of Malawi, 2000:5). The reasoning was that this would allow the 'enhancement of the management of performance by managers and [of] policy-making capacity' by political leaders (Government of Malawi, 1996:10). Durevall and Erlandsson (2005:15) note that the attractive performance-based salaries were supposed to provide incentives for controlling officers not to overrun their budgets and to withstand ministers' desire to overspend. As a result, an improvement was expected in 'planning, resourcing, monitoring, management and accounting systems so that resources are more sharply focused on priorities and public expenditure is more effectively controlled' (Government of Malawi 1996:3). The vision was to create 'an affordable, highly motivated, productive, professional and result oriented public service' that would 'deliver services to the public in an efficient, effective and responsible manner in order to satisfy national aspirations and promote the growth of wealth creating private sector' (Government of Malawi 2002:11). The need was 'to design and implement organisation and staffing structures and management systems which enable ministries and departments to achieve their objectives efficiently' (Government of Malawi 1996:3).

In line with the dictates of NPM, the performance-contracting scheme in Malawi had performance targets that public managers were expected to achieve, with the success of managers being measured against those targets. Below we discuss in more detail the performance targets, measures and contract-related rewards and punishments, as enshrined in the *Performance Management Handbook for the Malawi Civil Service*, on which the performance-contracting system was based

Performance Contracting Targets

Leadership Targets
The first set of targets was concerned with leadership. For contract employees to excel, they had to show that they were creative and had a clear vision, were able to initiate and manage change in the pursuit of strategic objectives and maintained high standards of integrity, honesty and drive in their work. The maximum score for this target was 10 points.

Managing People
This performance target entailed being able to develop staff to meet challenging organisational needs, to make use of skills and resources within a team, to build trust, good morale and team work and to secure commitment to change through appropriate involvement of staff. The maximum score for this target was 10 points.

Managing Financial Resources
In terms of the management of financial resources, employees had to demonstrate that they could secure value for money, negotiate for the resources to do the job in the light of wider priorities and commit and re-align resources to meet key priorities. The maximum score for this target was 10 points.

Strategic Thinking and Planning
The targets for strategic thinking and planning included developing and influencing strategic aims in anticipation of future demands, opportunities and threats, demonstrating sensitivity to the ministry's needs and wider environmental issues and translating strategic aims into practical and achievable plans. The maximum score for this target was 5 points.

Delivery of Results
With regard to delivery, managers had to be able to make quality decisions on time and with integrity, define results in relation to stakeholders' needs, manage relationships with customers/stakeholders effectively, organise work processes to deliver on time and/or on budget and to agreed quality standards, strive for continuous performance improvements while encouraging others to do the same and monitor performance and incorporate feedback in future plans. The maximum score for this target was 5 points.

Communication and Interpersonal Skills

In the area of communication and interpersonal skills, managers were supposed to show they were capable of negotiating effectively and handling hostility, being concise and persuasive both orally and in writing, listening with sensitivity to others' reactions; and building, maintaining and using an effective network of contacts. The maximum score for this target was 5 points.

Expertise and Professional Competence

Expertise and professional competence were measured by managers' ability to accept personal responsibility for the quality of their work, give professional advice to others, ensure that decisions were informed by relevant specialists or experts and influence decisions through the depth and breadth of their expertise. The maximum score for this target was 5 points.

Intellect, Creativity and Judgment

Managers deemed to have high degrees of intellect, creativity and judgment had to demonstrate the ability to focus on key issues and principles, follow a creative and constructive approach to solving problems, offer insights and generate original ideas with a practical approach, analyse ambiguous data and concepts rigorously, display confidence in their own judgement while also responding constructively to alternative ideas and encourage ideas, initiatives and innovations. The maximum score for this target was 5 points.

Personal Effectiveness

The last target was concerned personal effectiveness. To demonstrate this quality, one had to be able to adapt quickly and flexibly to new demands, manage time well to meet competing priorities, take a firm stand when circumstances warranted, be aware of personal strengths and weaknesses, show commitment to one's personal and professional impact on others and pursue adopted strategies with energy and commitment. The maximum score for this target was 5 points.

Performance Measurement and Outcomes

Performance was measured using five "levels", as shown in table 4.1 below, and an aggregate overall performance score calculated.

Table 4.1: Performance Rating

Grades	Rating Levels	Description
Outstanding	Level 5	Exceeds expectations and objectives
Very Good	Level 4	Achieves objectives and expectations
Good	Level 3	Meets most objectives and expectations
Satisfactory	Level 2	Barely meets most objectives and expectations
Unsatisfactory	Level 1	Does not meet objectives and expectations

Source: Adapted from Government of Malawi 2000

Based on the aggregate performance score, managers would then be offered contract-related rewards or sanctions as shown in table 4.2 below.

Table 4.2: Performance Rewards and Sanctions

Grades and Levels	Recommended Rewards	Recommended Sanctions
Outstanding (Level 5)	• Distinguished Award • Recommendation for promotion • Opportunity to renew contract	None
Very Good (Level 4)	• Recommendation for promotion • Opportunity to renew contract	None
Good (Level 3)	• Opportunity to renew contract	Recommendation for improvement
Satisfactory (Level 2)	• Negotiated opportunity to renew contract	Recommendation for significant improvement
Unsatisfactory (Level 1)	• None	Recommendation for termination of contract

Source: Adapted from Government of Malawi 2000

Performance Contracting in Malawi: A Failed Experiment?

Performance contracting in Malawi was trumpeted as a key instrument for the attainment of public-sector efficiency and effectiveness. This was in line with the African Development Fund's position (2004:5) that performance contracting leads to 'increased efficiency as the senior staff takes advantage of better incentives in exchange for greater accountability in terms of agreed upon results'. In practice, however, the challenges faced by the performance management scheme in Malawi were so huge that the government abandoned the scheme altogether and went back to the traditional pensionable system in May 2007. The abandonment of performance contracting affirms Islam's observation (1993, cited in Turner and Hulme 1997:190) that performance contracts are 'theoretically sound' but practically unattainable.

The first problem with the performance-contracting scheme in Malawi is that it was adopted too quickly (Durevall and Erlandsson 2005:15). It was implemented in haste, without regard to the specific social, cultural and economic conditions it was to operate in. In addition, there was not much background preparation in terms of putting in place the required institutions for the effective implementation of the scheme. For instance, the World Bank (2003:21) notes that employees on the contract system had 'not been linked to their correct salary grades thus leading to erroneous salary payments' (World Bank 2003:21). Moreover, the performance contracts did not enjoy institutional support, as many employees did not want to be evaluated. Many public managers 'hesitated for fear of unfair performance appraisals' (Durevall 2001:13). Durevall and Erlandsson (2005:15) argue that performance evaluations were not in the interest of the majority of senior public officials, while Fozzard and Simwaka (2002:12) note that the performance targets were 'vaguely couched' and difficult to measure. No reliable instruments for performance measurement were available.

At a deeper level, effective performance contracts require 'investment in skilled personnel, training, and introduction of a culture of innovative professionalism' (Turner and Hulme 1997:190). However, in Malawi, some officers on contract did not have the requisite qualifications and skills to meet the required performance targets. Promotion had not been based on qualifications but on experience and length of service. As a result, some public managers did not have the managerial expertise to achieve the efficiency goals. Even those who had good skills could not perform effectively and with a clear sense of creativity, intellect, innovation and judgment, because 'senor civil servants in many cases lacked sufficient control over their own organisation to actually be held responsible for the financial results' (World Bank 2003:53). One senior officer pointed out that 'in government, one has to work within policy guidelines and political considerations, so that the whole idea of discretion is rather difficult'.

Another major challenge concerned the sustainability of the performance-contract system. Turner and Hulme (1997:190) note that performance contracts work by motivating personnel through financial incentives. In Malawi, the new system resulted in dramatic increases in the salaries of the public officers who participated. Durevall (2001:13) estimates that these pay level increases were about 500 per cent. Valentine (2003, cited in Durevall and Erlandsson 2005:16) notes that public officers on contract, although comprising only 0.4 per cent of all civil servants, accounted for 6.8 per cent of the total wage bill. Those on contract ended up receiving the same salaries as top civil servants in Botswana, a country that has 18 times the GDP of Malawi, and far higher salaries than their counterparts in countries in the region with similar GDP (Valentine 2003). These salaries put huge pressure on the government wage bill, and, as a result, the performance scheme brought 'anxiety regarding the sustainability of the system itself' (Durevall 2001:13).

The problem of high salary costs was also cited as the reason for not extending performance contracts to middle or lower levels of management. However, this created another problem. It was found that middle-level and low-level managers are precisely the ones that required the contract system, because they are the officers most responsible for the actual performance of the public sector. In most cases, top civil servants only carry out ceremonial duties rather than hands-on management. Moreover, as Fozzard and Simwaka (2002:12) point out, senior staff are at the end of their careers. They are unlikely to resign in search of higher levels of pay, and their performance is dependent on that of lower-level staff anyway. Thus, as Durevall (2001:13) notes, 'initially only those close to retirement accepted performance based contracts'. Performance contracts also encouraged laziness and laxity by lower-level managers, many of whom thought there was no need to perform as they were not bound by a contract. According to the Principal Secretary in the Department of Human Resources and Development, 'the performance related contract scheme created an impression that it was only top management employees who were required to perform' (Daily Times, 12 June 2007). Moreover, the performance-contracting scheme was voluntary. All public officers eligible for contract employment had the option to be on the contract scheme or not. This meant the application of double standards. It implied that public servants who did not opt for performance contracts would not be expected to perform, while other public officials on the same level and grade who go for the contract scheme would be expected to perform very highly or lose their jobs. The result was generally uncoordinated and disjointed performance in the public sector. In addition, performance contracting distorted the salary structure of public servants. It increased the salary gap between the highest-paid employees and the rest. As a result, 'a small number of senior officials [were] ... very highly paid by regional standards, while salaries at lower levels [were] much more modest' (Claussen et al. 2006:9), thereby creating an 'unusual pattern of remuneration' (Claussen et al, 2006:9). The abandonment of the performance contract therefore has been seen as an attempt to compress the salary structure.

Another important reason for the failure of performance contracting in Malawi was political. Many of those who did not opt for performance contracts based their decision on fears that the system would be abused by powerful political interests, and, indeed, performance contracting was subject to political abuse.

Some managers' contracts were terminated on political grounds rather than for lack of performance. Many public managers 'hesitated for fear of unfair performance appraisals' (Durevall 2001:13), a common reaction in the event of a change in government administration. Experience has shown that it is easier for senior government officers on contract to be removed from office, especially when they are perceived not to align with the ruling party or to be sympathetic to the opposition parties. The government can hide under the cover of "non-performance" when the actual reasons for non-renewal are political. Moreover, such decision are difficult to appeal, as the performance measures are highly subjective. The performance-based contract scheme in Malawi was criticized for being used as a political instrument of patronage to manipulate the bureaucracy for political gains. Khembo (2004:285) points out that most people on contract were 'party loyalists ... [who were] awarded hefty packages through patronage' (Khembo 2004:285). For Khembo (2004:285), the aim of performance-based contracts was 'to politically neutralize the pervasive influence of permanent secretaries who had been appointed by the Malawi Congress Party (MCP) regime without dismantling them but by adding the known supporters of United Democratic Front (UDF) to this cadre'. The underlying aim was to gain 'extra- constitutional control of the state decision making machinery' (Khembo 2004:285).

Finally, public officials resented contract-based employment because of a favourable cultural orientation toward pensionable employment. This orientation is to earn less salary now in order to enjoy a better pension on retirement. The new system reversed this basic orientation, which may be why, as Durevall (2001:13) notes, 'only those close to retirement accepted performance based contracts since they since had little to lose'.

Conclusion

NPM reforms have been trumpeted as both universally applicable and effective in attaining higher levels of efficiency and effectiveness in the delivery of public goods and services. This paper, however, has shown that there is no such thing as a master key in performance management, because successful implementation of NPM-related tools depends on the country-specific environment. In the case of Malawi, although NPM-based performance-contract measures were put in place in order to achieve staffing structures and management systems that would enable ministries and departments to achieve their objectives more efficiently, Malawi simply does not have a conducive social, economic, political or cultural environment for the successful implementation of the system. As a result, the performance- contracting scheme failed, and the government abandoned it.

References

African Development Fund, 2004, *Republic of Malawi Support for Good Governance Loan Appraisal Report*, Johannesburg: African Development Fund.

Claussen J., Amis P., Delay S. and McGrath J., 2006, *Joint Evaluation of General Budget Support 1994-2004 Malawi Country Report*, Birmingham: University of Birmingham.

Daily Times, 2007, 'Government Reverses PSs' Service Conditions', 12 June.

Durevall, D., 2001, 'Reform of the Malawian Public Sector: Incentives, Governance and Accountability', Wider Discussion Paper no. 2001/109.

Durevall, D. and Erlandsson M., 2005, *Public Finance Management Reform in Malawi*, SIDA Country Economic Report 1.

Economic Commission for Africa, 2003, *Public Sector Management Reforms in Africa: Lessons Learned*, Addis Ababa: Economic Commission for Africa.

Fozzard, A. and Simwaka, C., 2002, *How, When and Why Does Poverty Get Budget Priority? Poverty Reduction Strategy and Public Expenditure in Malawi*, Overseas Development Institute, Case Study 4, Working Paper 166.

Hood, C., 1991, 'A Public Management for All Seasons?', *Public Administration*, Vol. 69, pp. 3-19.

Khembo, S.N., 2004, 'The Constitution, Constitutionalism and Democracy in Malawi: The Reign of Parliamentary Oligarchy', in A. Nhema, ed., *The Quest for Peace in Africa*, OSSREA: Addis Ababa, pp. 269-295.

Government of Malawi, 1996, *Action Plan for Civil Service Reform*, Office of President and Cabinet: Lilongwe.

Government of Malawi, 2000, *Performance Management Handbook for the Malawi Civil Service*, Lilongwe: Government Press.

Government of Malawi, 2002, *Public Sector Reform Programme 2002-2006: Programme Support Document*, Lilongwe, Government Press.

Minogue, M, 1998, 'Changing the State: Concepts and Practice in the Reform of the Public Sector", in M. Minogue, C. Polidano and D. Hulme, eds., *Beyond the New Public Management: Changing Ideas and Practices in Governance*, Cheltenham: Edward Elgar, pp. 17-37.

Osborn, D. and Gaebler, T., 1992, *Reinventing Government: How the Entrepreneurial Spirit is Transforming Government*, Oxford: Oxford University Press.

Polidano, C., Hulme, D. and Minogue, M., 1998, 'Conclusions: Looking Beyond the New Public Management', in M. Minogue, C. Polidano and D. Hulme, *Beyond the New Public Management: Changing Ideas and Practices in Governance*, Cheltenham: Edward Elgar, pp 278-293.

Tambulasi, R.I.C., 2007, 'Who Is Fooling Who? New Public Management Oriented Management Accounting and Political Control in Malawi's Local Governance', *Journal of Accounting and Organisational Change*, Vol. 3, Issue 3, pp. 302-328.

Turner, M. and Hulme, D., 1997, *Governance, Administration and Development: Making the State Work*, London: Macmillan.

World Bank, 2003, *Malawi Country Finance Accountability Assessment*, Washington DC: World Bank.

5

Resurrecting the Developmental State in Malawi: Reflections and Lessons from the 2005/2006 Fertiliser Subsidy Programme

Blessings Chinsinga

Introduction

Malawi has experienced two distinct phases of development. The first phase spanned the years from the attainment of independence in July 1964 to the end of the 1970s. The second phase began with the adoption of structural adjustment programmes (SAPs) in 1981(Chipeta 1993; Chirwa 1997; Harrigan 2001; Chinsinga 2002). The first phase saw the country's economy registering very high growth rates and enjoying relatively favourable balance of payment positions. Almost every sector experienced rapid growth, and Malawi was characterised at one point a 'star performer' in Africa (Archaya 1978; World Bank 1982). In stark contrast, the post-1979 phase witnessed almost every sector of the economy experiencing a decline followed by erratic recovery trends of the boom-and-bust type (Kaluwa et al. 1992; Chirwa 1995; Chilowa et al. 2003).

Several scholars have argued that the characterisation of Malawi's economy as a star performer was a glaring misdiagnosis of the underlying dynamics of the country's political economy at that time. Contrary to the World Bank's view, Malawi was not a paragon of a free-market, non-interventionist capitalist economy. The tremendously rapid economic growth that the country registered during the early decades of independence was very much state-driven, akin to the patterns observed in the context of the newly industrialising countries (NICs) (Pryor 1990; Harrigan 2001). Thus, Mhone (1987) argues that 'the logic of Malawi's economic policy ... [lay] in the government's ability to manipulate wage policy, labour flows, agricultural price and subsidization policies, and monetary policies to the maximization of forced savings which [were] ... directed into productive investment' (cited in Harrigan 2001:39). The major difference between the NICs and

Malawi experience, however, was that the latter's growth was generated by the agricultural rather than the industrial sector.

This early success story became hollow as soon as the state-driven development strategy could not be sustained. In Harrigan's words, by 1980, 'it was obvious that the intricate relationships between Malawi's corporate, parastatal, and banking sectors, used by President Banda to foster the estate boom of the 1970s, were no longer sustainable' (Harrigan, 2001:43). This, in turn, exposed the chronic structural imbalances and rigidities of the economy and progressively undermined Malawi's creditworthiness, prompting it to seek the intervention of the World Bank and IMF. The Bretton Woods institutions prescribed structural adjustment programmes (SAPs) as a remedial measure for the country's economic predicament, but, since then, the economy has been unstable, experiencing boom-and-bust growth patterns underpinned by rising levels of inflation, declining agricultural productivity, rising interest rates and spirals in both domestic and external debt (Kaluwa et al. 1992; Jenkins and Tsoka 2003; Chinsinga 2007a). In short, SAPs failed to alter the structure of the economy but instead exacerbated its vulnerability, which has been compounded by frequent droughts and flooding in recent years. One of the most notable consequences of the adverse impact of SAPs was that in the period between 1989 and 2004, Malawi was unable to meet its national food requirements without having to import maize or seeking food aid, even in years of good rains.

This situation has been turned around since the introduction of the fertiliser subsidy scheme in the 2005/2006 growing season. The programme ensured that, in 2006, Malawi enjoyed its biggest-ever harvest of 2.6 million metric tonnes, at least half a million tones more than its annual food requirements of two million tonnes. The surplus for the 2006/2007 growing season has more than doubled (Chinsinga 2007b).

This paper explores whether the experiences leading to the adoption and successful implementation of the 2005/2006 fertiliser subsidy programme can be exploited as the basis for creating a viable framework for a developmental state in Malawi, broadly understood as a state that seriously attempts to deploy its administrative and political resources to the task of economic development. The fertiliser subsidy programme is the most significant developmental policy achievement the government since the advent of a democratic political dispensation over a decade ago, especially in view of the fact that the programme was implemented against the advice of technical experts and development partners.

The Developmental State in Perspective

Scholarly debate about the developmental state is as old as the discipline of development studies itself. In fact, according to some scholars, this debate has now come full circle (Chikulo 1998; Mkandawire 1998; Bull 2006). At the dawn of the first development decade in the 1950s, there was unshakeable faith in the ability of the state to spearhead development as a mobiliser of resources, provider of infrastructure and public entrepreneur advancing the pace of economic growth and development. The state was given a central role in the pioneering views of the process of development (Sanbrook 1993:Mkandawire 1998). However, the economic crisis of the late 1970s and early 1980s changed all this. From being glorified as a catalyst of development, the state was firmly condemned as the major impediment to the achievement of rapid and sustainable economic growth and development in the developing world. A litany of pejoratives describing the state became fashionable;[1] and the state became 'the most demonized institution, vilified for its weakness, its overextension, its repressive character, its ubiquity, its absence etc.' (Mkandawire 1998:1).

Through its diagnosis of the development constraints facing developing countries published in the famous 1981 Berg Report, the World Bank prescribed SAPs as an effective panacea to resuscitate economic growth and development in these countries (World Bank 1989; Chikulo 1998; Cammack 2002; Simon 2002). SAPs substantially rolled back the involvement of the state in the development processes against the backdrop of a dogmatic advocacy of market reforms. Simply stated, SAPs advocated for the withdrawal of the state which, in turn, led not only to the weakening of the state but also the downscaling of its size and influence (Chikulo 1998; Mkandawire 1998). The faith pinned on the market as an alternative institutional framework for spearheading development soon degenerated into disappointment, however. The most familiar conclusion of evaluation studies is that SAPs were associated with a huge drop in living standards and a huge rise in inequalities. SAPs generated adverse socio-economic effects and considerably weakened the state and its internal structures. Unemployment and the prices of essential commodities soared, while expenditures on social services, especially health and education, substantially declined (Clark 1991; Chipeta 1993; Chinsinga 2003a). Ultimately, SAPs greatly debilitated the role of the state in the socio-economic development process necessary for rapid and sustainable economic recovery.

The disappointing track record of the SAPs invariably brought the role of the state back into the limelight in development discourse. This trend was further enhanced by the debate about the historically remarkable success story of the Newly Industrialising Countries, popularly dubbed the East Asian miracle (Chinsinga 2003b; Bull 2006). Led by the World Bank, the neo-liberals argued that the success of the NICs was indebted to the market-oriented policies these countries had put in place. The argument was that such policies encouraged investments and exports that, in turn, contributed towards remarkable economic growth and development. The alternative view was that the East Asian miracle should be attributed to strategic state intervention. The advocates of this view contended that the key to the success of the NICs was that they provided state incentives selectively to increase productivity in the private sector (Amsden 1989; Bull 2006).

The weight of evidence marshalled by the advocates of the role of the state in the NIC success story opened a new epoch in discussions of the developmental state. Popularly characterised as "bringing the state back in", these discussions were relaunched by the World Bank in its 1997 *World Development Report*, in which it unequivocally acknowledged, for the first time since the 1981 Berg Report, that the state had a key role to play in socio-economic development. The bank's position tremendously amplified the UNDP position adopted a year earlier. Read together, the UNDP and the World Bank advocated for the reinvigoration of state institutions and capabilities if people's needs were to be effectively addressed. Thus, the two institutions acknowledged the need for a strong activist state. The UNDP specifically pointed out that 'a poverty eradication strategy requires not a retreating, weak state but an active, strong one, and the strength should be used to enable the poor rather than disable them' (UNDP 1996:101).

With the debate about developmental states rekindled, the key question remains: what *is* a developmental state? This is not as straightforward a question as it may seem. The main challenge in defining a developmental state is the tendency to equate it with impressive economic performance (Mkandawire 1998), since the evidence for a developmental state is often drawn deductively from the performance of the economy. But this overlooks the possibility that economic failure may not be a consequence of the lack of genuine developmental commitments and efforts by the state. The government's political and technical capacity may simply not be enough to fend off exogenous forces. According to Mkandawire (1998), the preoccupation with economic performance as a yardstick for defining a developmental state risks, among other things, rendering the resulting definitions tautological.

Scholars often have recourse to the NICs in their attempts to define a developmental state (Chikulo 1998; Harrigan 2001; Mbabazi and Taylor 2005; Bull 2006). From this perspective, a developmental state is generally defined as one whose ideological underpinnings are developmental and that seriously attempts to deploy its administrative and political resources to the task of economic development. Thus, a state qualifies as developmental if it is purposefully driven to promote development and utilise its offices in order to facilitate improvement alongside other actors such as the private sector and civil society (Mbabazi and Taylor 2005). The definition of a developmental state offered by Leftwich (1995) deserves to be specially highlighted, however. Leftwich (1995) defines developmental states as those whose politics have concentrated sufficient power, autonomy and capacity at the centre to shape, pursue and encourage the achievement of explicit developmental objectives, whether by establishing and promoting the conditions and direction of economic growth or by organising it directly, or by a combination of both. The uniqueness of Leftwich's definition lies in its emphasis that the pace and thrust of state developmental strategies must be politically driven and shaped (see also Chikulo 1998; Mbabazi and Taylor 2005).

Mkandawire's (1998) analytical deconstruction of the concept of a developmental state ties together Leftwich's perspective and the popular conception of the developmental state as stated above. He points out that the developmental state has two dimensions: ideological and structural. A state is ideologically developmental if it conceives its mission as one of ensuring economic development, usually interpreted to mean high rates of accumulation and industrialisation. It is structurally developmental if it has the capacity to implement its economic policies effectively. This capacity is dependent on a whole range of institutional, technical, administrative and political factors. Nevertheless, a number of distinct features of the developmental state can be isolated (Leftwich 1995; Mkandawire 1998; Mbabazi and Taylor 2005). These include:

- existence of a determined developmental elite who are legitimate and capable and are backed up by a competent and insulated bureaucracy;

- autonomy of the state from social forces so that it can use its capacities to devise long-term economic policies unencumbered by myopic special interests;

- social anchoring that prevents the state from using its autonomy in a predatory manner and enables it to mainatin the support of key social actors:

- a bureaucracy with integrity and the capacity to make decisions for the benefit of society as a whole, rather than favouring specific groups:

- a political milieu where this bureaucracy has enough space to operate and take policy initiatives independent of overly intrusive interventions by vested interests:

- effective methods of state intervention in the economy without sabotaging the market principle.

Malawi's Experience with the Developmental State

Malawi has experienced two distinct political periods since independence in July 1964. Until May 1994, Malawi was a one-party authoritarian state led by Dr Kamuzu Banda under the auspices of the Malawi Congress Party (MCP). Malawi then became a plural polity following the May 1994 general elections that saw the ascendancy of the United Democratic Front (UDF) at the helm of government (Chinsinga 2003c; Dulani 2005). The one-party state had become a developmental disaster, since the state was dominated by a small ruling clique led by Banda, Mama Cecilia Kadzamira and John Tembo, characterised by Mhone (1992) as the governing triumvirate at the apex of an autocratic state machinery.

Nearly all accounts of one-party Malawi characterise it as a complete betrayal of the spirit of the independence struggle (Nzunda and Ross 1995). Independence had been greeted as an opportunity to redress popular grievances, promote economic development and generally rescue Malawi from the junk heap of colonial history, where it had been relegated to the status of a colonial slum (Mhone 1987; Kishindo 1997). However, foreshadowed by the 1964 cabinet crisis, a political environment capable of fulfilling the dreams of the independence struggle failed to materialise. The ministerial and parliamentary structures of the new state were purely nominal and had the facile function of rubber stamping and rationalising handed down policies. Consequently, the state became an 'executive committee of the dominant, but minority, economic interests consisting of indigenous commercial farmers, distribution and retail entrepreneurs, the political elite, top bureaucrats and the top management in statutory bodies' (Mhone 1992:5).

Characterising this one-party regime as a developmental state would be ludicrous. Despite its name, the *Statement of Development Policies*, the key policy blueprint for the regime until its demise in May 1994, was only a framework to enable the ruling class to exploit the masses (Kishindo 1997; Ngwira 2002). Within this framework, agriculture, especially estate agriculture, was viewed as the generator of revenue to fuel investment in other sectors. The expenditure on the social sector was justified only to the extent that it served the purposes of economic growth. The assumption was that growth would expand aggregate human choice and, therefore, make positive contributions to the welfare of the people. The fight against poverty was considered to be more or less an automatic component of the *Statement of Development Policies*, perhaps inspired by the tenets of the trickle-down theoretical construct that was in its prime at that time (Kishindo 1997; Harrigan 2001). However, the lucrative estate agriculture prioritised in the *Statement of Development Policies* mostly just benefited a minority and functioned as an important instrument of patronage for Banda and the ruling clique, combined with coercion, charisma and populism. It is not surprising, therefore, that Malawi entered the 1990s as one of the poorest countries in the world, with widespread, severe and extremely deep levels of poverty. Life expectancy was in decline, infant, under-five and maternal mortality rates were alarmingly high, very few people had access to clean water and sanitary facilities and almost two-thirds of the population was illiterate.

The advent of democracy in May 1994 was celebrated as a momentous occasion signifying a new and inherently positive beginning in the country's development efforts. Oddly, however, the transition from authoritarian one-party rule to multiparty democracy is widely considered as marking the collapse of the country's policy-making processes (Rakner et al. 2004; Booth et al. 2006). The quality of policy and the policy-making capacity of the Malawi state rapidly deteriorated. In other words, the government's capacity for policy formulation and implementation became thin, and in some cases, virtually non-existent, resulting in a complete loss of direction for state business. This was surprising to say the least; the advent of a democracy had been expected to strengthen the quality and the capacity of policy-making processes, since the policy-making processes would now be subjected to the influence of a multitude of actors at various levels of society as part of the democratic process. Policy-making was also expected to be procedurally more open and inclusive, with qualitatively superior policy outcomes than in the past (Chinsinga 2007b). In the one-party regime, policy-making had been centralised in the presidency. The president had driven the vision, direction and pace of policy outcomes, especially in terms of defining the core ideas, framing the issues and setting the measures of success for policy initiatives.

It is, therefore, a huge paradox that, instead of improving, the quality of policy and policy-making greatly deteriorated (Rakner et al. 2004; Sahley et al. 2005; Booth et al. 2006). All accounts attribute the deterioration to the leadership and governance style of President Muluzi. Booth et al. (2006) provide the most elaborate account of the dynamics that decimated the capacity of the government machinery in the policy-making process. They argue that, unlike in the one-party regime, Muluzi and most of his ministers surrounded themselves with cronies, sidelining senior officials in a way that demotivated them and debilitated administrative capacity. This practice corrupted the civil service to the extent of undermining its capacity to generate coherent, well-grounded policy approaches. The civil service came to be dominated by presidential loyalists who were not competent to make use of technically orientated policy analysis. Thus, when technical advice was offered, it was not taken seriously. Technical specialists with evidence-based policy experience became progressively demotivated and adopted a *laissez-faire* approach to government business.

These developments were a radical departure from the one-party regime's policy-making processes. In Banda's regime, technical advice was seriously considered before being sidestepped. Instead of just being ignored, technical advice was only overruled after careful thought and consideration. Under Muluzi, the relatively honest, disciplined, well-paid, professional and hardworking civil service of the one-party era was replaced by a lax, demoralised and underpaid civil service distracted by private business activities and more easily corrupted. Coupled with Muluzi's lack of a clear and articulated development vision for Malawi, this created a situation in which policy was driven mainly by patronage, in sharp contrast to the previous regime where patronage had followed policy. According to Booth et al. (2006), Banda's long-term vision during the one-party era combined with a professional and well functioning civil service to ensure that policy was made and implemented with a degree of consistency.

The decline in the government's capacity to formulate and implement policy is ironically underscored by the multiplicity of grand policy documents published since the turn of the 1990s. According to Booth et al. (2006), a notable feature of Malawi's situation is the plethora of policy documents on the one hand, and the absence of successfully implemented policies on the other hand. At least five grand policy documents have been produced since 1994, but compared to the policies of the 1960s and 1970s, which lived through their planning horizon, the recent policy documents have all overlapped. This, in turn, has created considerable policy uncertainties and made policy coherence extremely difficult to achieve (Chirwa, Kydd and Doward 2006). The challenges created by these fluid, shifting policy strategies were duly recognised in the 2002-2006 Public Sector Management Reform Programme (PSMRP). The PSMRP acknowledged that the policy-making processes in Malawi are chaotic because of the absence of a central agency charged with the responsibility of providing leadership and creating public support for policy reforms and initiatives.

Policy-making in Malawi has therefore largely been on an ad hoc basis. In many ways, donors have greatly contributed to the crisis situation in the policy-making realm in the country. An increasing number of donors have taken advantage of the weakened or virtually non-existent technical capacity to coordinate policy formulation in government to step into the vacuum to the extent that oftentimes decisions taken by donors have effectively settled policy. The main problem has been that the donor approaches to the policy-making function have equally not been immune to short-termism, competitiveness and personality politics characteristic of state policy (cf. Harrigan 2005; Sahley et al. 2005). Consequently, competing views, interests and demands among donors have substantially compromised policy coherence, and subjected policy-making and implementation to often polarised ideological leanings and orientations. In some cases, projects or policy initiatives were identified with specific individuals within the donor agencies, which posed serious problems of consistency and continuity when their tenure of office expired (Booth et al. 2006). In short, donors made matters worse by their fragmented, ad hoc and sometimes confrontational stance in discharging policy functions.

There are, however, some signs of recovery regarding the government's capacity to formulate, articulate and implement credible policy interventions. President Bingu wa Mutharika, who succeeded Bakili Muluzi in 2004, is restoring and championing a fairly technocratic approach to policy-making patterned on an elaborate development vision for the country.[2] This vision is underpinned by the Malawi Growth and Development Strategy (MGDS), touted as an overarching policy framework for wealth creation and economic growth as a means of reducing poverty sustainably. The MGDS distinguishes five thematic areas: sustainable economic growth, social protection, social development, infrastructure development and improved governance. The major sign of the country's recovery in the realm of policy-making is the successful implementation of the fertiliser subsidy programme in the 2005/2006 growing season. At the same time, doubts have been expressed as to whether Mutharika's politics will be significantly different from those of his predecessors. The argument is that he might have a genuine desire to transform the way government works but that his efforts are likely to be undermined by the realities of Malawi's politics. Patronage is deeply entrenched and embedded as an organising framework for politics in the country, and any kind of radical reforms will have contend with its enduring logic (Sahley et al. 2005; Booth et al. 2006).

Context and Origins of the 2005/2006 Fertiliser Subsidy Programme

The origins of the fertiliser subsidy programme can be traced to the electoral campaign for the May 2004 elections that saw the election of President Mutharika on a United Democratic Front (UDF) ticket. The distinctive feature of the 2004 electoral campaign was that it reflected a strong national consensus for fertiliser subsidy, as all leading candidates promised some kind of support to the smallholder agricultural sector. This was not surprising, given that the problem of food security had become more or less endemic in the country since the 1990s. Recurrent episodes of severe hunger crises had turned food security into a fierce battleground both for parties in government and outside government.

Two broad positions on fertiliser subsidy could be distinguished during the campaign. The ruling UDF and its coalition partners advocated a universal fertiliser subsidy for maize producers only. They promised to reduce the price of fertiliser from MK 3,000 to MK 1,500 per 50kg bag. The opposition block, led by the MCP, advocated a universal fertiliser subsidy programme for both maize and tobacco producers. Prices for both maize and tobacco fertilisers would be reduced to MK 950 per 50kg. The differences in the subsidy proposals reflected, to a large extent, the variations in the regional support bases for the political parties. The MCP, whose strongest political base (the central region) is a dominant tobacco producer, had no choice but to advocate extending the fertiliser subsidy programme to tobacco (Chirwa, Kydd and Doward 2006).

The hallmark for this electoral campaign was a simple narrative: hunger and recurrent food crises are best responded to by supporting agriculture, and this means providing subsidies to get agriculture moving with a focus on key crops. National food security and a reduction on the dependence on food imports required, it was argued, concrete state action. The basic argument in this narrative was that Malawi ought to be self-sufficient in food production. This cannot be left to chance, the argument went, since it costs much more for the country to import food than to grow its own, especially when foreign exchange reserves are not always readily available. Besides, food imports often arrive too late, stay too long and get enmeshed in politics, while donor aid is unpredictable (Bird, Booth and Pratt 2003; Levy 2005).

The UDF won the May 2004 elections. The popular expectation was that the new government would immediately reduce fertiliser prices as promised during the campaign period. This did not happen. Indeed, the government took a very long period of time to even articulate a clear and concrete fertiliser policy (Chimphonda and Dzoole-Mwale 2005). The delay in clarifying the government's position created the impression that there would be a universal fertiliser subsidy, which turned out not to be the case. Instead of implementing a fertiliser subsidy programme, the government announced in August 2005 that it would continue with the Targeted Input Programme (TIP), but on a much bigger scale. This programme provided at least half of farming families with free inputs containing 0.1 ha worth of fertiliser, maize seed and legume seed. The expanded version of TIP (ETIP) was made available to 2.1 million farming families – a significant increase over the 1.5 million targeted in the regular TIP, but falling short of the implied promise made earlier of cheap fertiliser for everyone (Sahley et al. 2005). The uncertainty was further enhanced when the Principal Secretary of Agriculture, speaking at the annual meeting of the National Smallholder Farmers Association, hinted that fertiliser prices would go down and advised farmers to wait before procuring fertilisers until government had come up with a definite statement on prices (Nation 2004).

The uncertainty had two serious consequences for the 2004/2005 growing season. First, it made it extremely difficult for the private sector to make orders for fertiliser on a timely basis. This led to a scarcity of fertiliser on the market, even for those farmers who could afford the prevailing market prices. Second, the ETIP inputs arrived very late because of the time it takes to get fertiliser into the country from overseas suppliers. The delivery period for fertiliser is about 8 to 12 weeks from the time orders are placed with the suppliers. Consequently, the distribution of ETIP inputs was delayed, in most cases done after the maize had already developed past the critical stage for the application of basal dressing fertiliser (Sahley et al. 2005; Chimphonda and Dzoole-Mwale 2005). Coupled with a severe drought during the 2004/2005 growing season, this culminated in a severe hunger crisis affecting about four million Malawians. The food deficit was estimated in the region of 700,000-1,000,000 tonnes out of the 2.1 million metric tonne annual requirement.

It is argued that the government was hesitant to implement a universal fertiliser subsidy programme for fear of jeopardising the prospects of qualifying for debt relief under the Malawi Poverty Reduction Strategy (MPRS). The restoration of fiscal prudence and discipline was one of the key triggers for the country to qualify. At the peak of the 2004 campaign, donors had warned that increasing the fertiliser subsidy could affect the decision on the country's US$113 million debt. Moreover, donors had suspended aid to the country since 2001 due to problems that included: (1) diversion of donor resources to non-priority areas; (2) unbudgeted expenditures, especially on external travel; (3) disbursement of resources to the poor without a viable bureaucratic mechanism for accountability, and (4) a dramatic increase in official corruption and patronage (Fozzard and Simwaka 2002; Rakner et al. 2004).

The Battle for a Universal Fertiliser Subsidy Programme

The 2004/2005 hunger crisis intensified the debate about the need for the re-introduction of the fertiliser subsidy programme. In particular, it provided opposition political parties and advocacy groups with a platform to attack the president and his administration for failing to deliver on the promise made during the electoral campaign. They argued that the president had not only failed to reduce the prices of fertiliser but, perhaps more critically, had messed up the ETIP and thereby brought on the 2004/2005 hunger crisis (Sahley et al. 2005; IRIN 2007). The fact that the president had resigned from the UDF, the party that had sponsored him, and formed his own party, the Democratic Progressive Party (DDP), did not help matters. The main challenge for the president was that his newly formed party had weak representation in parliament, and his decision to ditch the UDF dramatically increased tensions in the political atmosphere.

The 2004/2005 hunger crisis also prompted the Parliamentary Committee on Agriculture and Natural Resources (PCANR) into action. Members of PCANR carried out a study that critically reviewed the food security situation, possible interventions and the status and prospects of agriculture in the country. The main recommendation of PCANR, dominated by the MCP, was that the country should introduce and implement a universal fertiliser subsidy for maize and tobacco. The justification was that it would address the market and productive sides of the food security equation respectively. PCANR's proposal was that price ranges for maize and tobacco fertilisers should be between MK 700 and MK 900 per 50kg (Chimphonda and Dzoole-Mwale 2005). However, the president's immediate response avoided any reference to the subsidy issue and suggested instead that the solution to Malawi's predicament lay in massive investment in irrigation, which past governments had neglected.

The president's response underlined his sensitivity to the concerns of donors. His main preoccupation at this time was to get the economy back on track by fixing key economic fundamentals. The previous administration had mismanaged the economy to the extent that, by 2004, it was on the brink of collapse. The president was determined, therefore, to win back donor confidence, so that the support donors had withdrawn in 2001 could be restored. The country was just beginning to get on course to achieve qualification for comprehensive debt relief, and the president did not want to jeopardise this. His response, however, did very little to shift the focus away from fertiliser subsidy as a potential remedy to the problem of food security in the country.

Meanwhile, DFID announced its withdrawal of support to TIP. DFID had been the major donor to the TIP programme since its introduction in the late 1990s and, by this time, DFID was the only remaining donor, the others having pulled out. Its timeframe for programme support had now expired, and programme appraisals had concluded that TIP was not the best way of offering support to the agricultural sector. Households targeted under TIP were the poorest of the poor (people with disabilities, the chronically sick, the elderly) and could not make productive use of the inputs. In most cases, the beneficiaries ended up either selling the inputs or not putting them to maximum productive use (Chinsinga, Dulani and Kayuni 2003; Levy 2005).

DFID's decision was another huge blow to Malawi's agricultural sector. Without TIP, the magnitude of food deficits would have been unbearable. This cannot be overemphasised, as Malawi's smallholder agriculture has not been without any kind of support since the removal of the fertiliser subsidy in the mid-1990s. In fact, recent trends show that, without any kind of support, the smallholder agricultural sector is almost non-viable. Most stakeholders interviewed emphasised that the majority of smallholders cannot afford the basic productive resources – seed and fertiliser – because of the severe poverty they find themselves in. Something, therefore, had to be done if Malawi was to avoid descending into an abyss of hunger. Moreover, a compact between government and its citizens regarding agricultural inputs entitlements seemed to be entrenched. This is aptly captured by Sahley et al. (2005:17):

> TIP failed to move households from subsistence to surplus production even under most suitable conditions: adequate rain and capable beneficiaries of properly applying the inputs. The condition of extreme poverty much of the population finds itself in has meant that fertiliser transfers have instead become part of most household subsistence strategies. Fertiliser transfers are no longer viewed as an effective livelihood development strategy. It has instead become a critical part of the national safety net. Fertiliser direct transfers or subsidies are now needed to keep households and communities from falling below the subsistence line.

For these reasons, and coupled with mounting pressure from the opposition parties, the president announced the introduction of a fertiliser subsidy programme in June 2005, emphasising that the subsidy would be targeted at resource-constrained but productive maize farmers. The objective of the programme was to provide fertiliser to people who had the resources to use it productively but would otherwise have difficulty in obtaining it. The architecture of the subsidy programme was based on lessons learnt from the implementation of TIP as observed above. The president ruled out a universal fertiliser subsidy programme as advocated by the PCANR, arguing that Malawi could not afford it. The president's more modest proposal would still cost between MK two and three billion. This guarded concession to the demand for a fertiliser subsidy was motivated by the president's desire not to alienate donors who were wary of the negative impact a universal fertiliser subsidy would have on the economy, notably on private sector development.

The proposal for a limited fertiliser subsidy ignited intense political debate. Opposition parties insisted on a universal programme and, taking advantage of their strength in parliament, made adoption of a universal programme a precondition for passing the 2005/2006 budget. The government gave in, and a universal fertiliser subsidy programme with a budget of MK 4.7 billion (about US$ 35 million) was agreed. The understanding of MPs was that any smallholder farmer would be entitled to buy as many bags of fertiliser as they could afford without any rationing mechanism in place. However, the programme was implemented using coupons.

Reactions to the Fertiliser Subsidy Programme

The implementation of the fertiliser subsidy programme against the backdrop of electoral, legislative and aid politics was seen in some quarters as a regressive and potentially disastrous step. Many technical experts and donors were appalled by the government's decision to go ahead with the subsidy programme. They argued that the programme ran counter to all the efforts at liberalisation reforms that had been ongoing for many years. The Economics Association of Malawi (ECAMA), for instance, argued that the implementation of the universal fertiliser subsidy would lead to economic disaster, since government would be forced to spend beyond its means. ECAMA pointed out that MPs were demanding a universal fertiliser subsidy without prescribing the source of funds and argued that a universal subsidy would force the government to borrow on the domestic market, which would then put pressure on inflation and interest rates. An additional concern of the technical experts and donors was that the government was implementing the programme without fully thinking about corresponding interventions to deal with marketing issues in case of a maize surplus. The argument was that, in the absence of such mechanisms, the subsidy programme risked creating disincentives to maize production, in which case the intended effect of the programme on food security would be negated. No donor supported the subsidy programme, and the full cost was borne by the government.

Ironically, this lack of donor support only reinforced the narrative that had been so prominent in the 2004 electoral campaign around the fertiliser subsidy programme and the achievement of food security. Notwithstanding the differences between the government and the opposition parties regarding the modalities of implementation, the consensus about the need for such a programme persisted strongly. The narrative was further embellished when it was argued that it was better to subsidize production than consumption. Experience with the 2004/2005 food crisis further solidified the narrative, particularly from the standpoint of the cost implications of importing food during a times of crisis. Food imports during the 2004/2005 crisis had cost MK13 billion, compared to the MK 4.7 billion proposed for the subsidy programme. This struck an instant chord with all segments of Malawian society; it was clear the fertiliser subsidy programme would be a more cost-effective approach to achieving food security than alternative interventions. Stambuli's study (2002), which argued that one dollar of food imports achieves only 30 per cent of what the same one dollar would have achieved as a production subsidy, was often invoked. Stambuli's study had been inspired by the observation that maize imports constituted the second largest budget item in Malawi after debt service. Stambuli (2002) estimated that a tonne of maize imports costs roughly US$ 300 and would feed five families for about 96 days. The same US$ 300, however, would be adequate to procure enough fertiliser to produce 13 tonnes of maize that would feed the same families for 10 months. A study by van Donge et al. (2002) found that farmers' cultivation of their own food crops is also highly valued culturally. A household that does not grow its own food is considered as good as dead.

Strikingly, the narrative around the subsidy programme rekindled the debate about whether or not to privatise ADMARC (Mvula, Chirwa and Kadzandira 2003; Chinsinga 2004). ADMARC, which in addition to holding a monopoly on farm inputs, was the sole trader of maize and the buyer of last resort. Its main function vis-à-vis food security was the maintenance of a maize price band. The aim of the price band was to stabilise prices and make maize affordable and accessible to the poorest Malawians by establishing floor prices to protect farmers' incomes and ceiling prices to protect consumers (Sahley et al. 2005; Chirwa, Kydd and Doward 2006). Instigated by the IMF and the World Bank under the auspices of structural adjustment programmes, ADMARC had been subjected to a number of reforms with a view to making it more efficient and effective. The rationale for the reforms was that ADMARC survived on heavy subsidies that drained the treasury and created disincentives for private-sector entry into the market. The reform measures had included management reforms, closure of uneconomic marketing outlets and liberalisation of smallholder farmer crops. But the closure of some uneconomic ADMARC markets substantially contributed to widespread food insecurity for smallholders, especially those in remote areas inaccessible to private traders. The strong national consensus around the fertiliser subsidy programme served as an occasion for stakeholders to campaign for the restoration of former ADMARC functions in the country's scheme of food security. This culminated in government setting aside MK 500 million for

ADMARC to buy surplus maize from farmers. This was justified as a strategy to avoid a repeat of the hunger that hit the country in 2004/2005. The former Minister of Agriculture summed the consensus: 'A nation that cannot feed itself cannot be a sovereign and independent state. We, in Malawi, must therefore be able to feed ourselves by whatever means' (Nation 2005).

Donors' Narratives of the Fertiliser Subsidy Programme

Donors were generally opposed to the subsidy programme when it was launched. However, they soon diverged into three distinct categories: those totally opposed to subsidies, those sceptical but willing to engage with subsidies (searching for the holy grail of "smart subsidies") and those supportive of subsidies. Most NGOs fall into the last category, although championing slightly different political and technical justifications and rationales for subsidies.

Donors Totally Opposed to Subsidies

The main donor agencies that remain entirely opposed to the subsidy programme include the International Monetary Fund (IMF) and the US Agency for International Development (USAID). The key argument of this group of donors is that subsidies create market distortions that make private-sector development virtually impossible (Harrigan 2005). They argue that the implementation of the subsidy programme risks wiping out the private sector dealing in fertiliser. This argument is justified on the basis that smallholder farmers' demand for fertiliser in Malawi is estimated at 200,000 metric tonnes per annum, while the subsidy programme provides up to 150,000 metric tonnes. However, the 150,000 metric tonne ceiling is likely to be exceeded due to excessive political pressure; it has, indeed, been reported that government printed 550,000 extra coupons over and above the initial number. There is evidence suggesting the private sector may be at risk of being crowded out. Until the turn of the 1990s, ADMARC was the sole outlet for fertilisers to the smallholder market. This changed following liberalisation, which opened up the market to private entrepreneurs. The shares of the private sector in both importation and sales have ever since remained over 70 per cent, at times peaking to over 90 per cent, until the introduction of the fertiliser subsidy in the 2005/2006 growing season. The share of the private sector in fertiliser importation has not been greatly affected compared to sales. While the private sector's share of sales in the 2004/2005 growing season stood at 168,576 tons (87%), its share declined to 92, 920 tons (41%) in the 2005/2006 growing season. It recovered to about 134,914 tons (52%) in the 2006/2007 growing season following the participation of the private sector in the distribution of subsidised fertiliser. This argument is further strengthened by Nakhumwa's (2005) observation that the fertiliser subsidy programme took up almost 91 per cent of the smallholder fertiliser market.

The agencies opposing the subsidy contend that the most effective way to boost agricultural development is to promote a market-based approach to input provision. They maintain that fertiliser subsidies are very difficult to target and that the benefits generally go to relatively well-off farmers. They argue that administrative costs, leakages and targeting problems make subsidies a grossly inefficient way to target the poor (Donovan 2004; Pender, Nkonya and Rosegrant 2004), while a market-based approach is ideal because it creates a favourable environment for the private sector to thrive and makes it easy for private-sector actors, and farmers themselves, to make sensible decisions about when to buy, at what prices and in what quantities. In particular, according to this view, uncertainty over government responses destabilises the market and dissuades the private sector from engaging in either fertiliser supply or grain trade, thereby keeping fertiliser expensive and unprofitable and output markets volatile.

Donors Sceptical but Willing to Engage with Subsidies

The group of donors sceptical but willing to engage with subsidies includes DFID, the World Bank and the EU, among others. These donors are wary about government capacity and emphasise the challenges of targeting. However, they concede that some type of "smart subsidy", building on the lessons of the targeted input programme, might be feasible. For this group, there is a clear case for subsidies in the case of market failure, but the subsidies should be properly targeted at economically active and productive beneficiaries. These donors are also interested in promoting private-sector development as the basis for economic growth. Subsidies are generally considered acceptable as long as they do not crowd out private-sector development. They are seen as short-term interventions but are considered fiscally unsustainable if the intention is to institutionalise subsidies as an integral part of a development strategy (Sahley et al. 2005). In this view, subsidies have to be conceived within the broader framework of social protection when market failures are rampant and the incidence of poverty and vulnerability is acute. In fact, recent studies by the World Bank and DFID have shown that poverty and vulnerability are deeply entrenched in Malawi, with about 52 per cent of the people living below the poverty line and 22.3 per cent ultra-poor. These people may require some kind of special intervention, since they are very unlikely to benefit from the process of economic growth (Government of Malawi/World Bank 2006; Devereux et al. 2006). The idea is to ensure that support is provided only to those that are genuinely unable to afford a certain commodity. Thus, these donors advocate for-targeted subsidiess with market-friendly mechanisms, subsidies that are clearly defined in terms of duration and financial commitments so as to ensure predictability. Since unpredictability would create excessive market distortions, they argue for clear exit strategies. From their point of view, subsidies are only a short-term intervention and are fiscally unsustainable in the long run.

At bottom, these agencies maintain that subsidies are not the best way to support agricultural development. They appeal to the experience of TIP to show that distribution of free inputs does not necessarily lead to enhanced production, arguing that people do not value free inputs and they do not use them optimally. Many TIP beneficiaries ended up selling their packs, for instance. Their argument, therefore, is that subsidies must be properly targeted and not run for more than five years before the beneficiaries graduate as self-reliant farmers. More generally, these donors – particularly the World Bank – see subsidies as a second-best option for revitalising smallholder agriculture. The argument is that other strategies are more effective than subsidies in ensuring small farmers can intensify production and adjust to market signals: efficient input distribution through publicly supported infrastructure, packaging standards, low-cost financial services, improved research and extension, new risk management mechanisms etc. Public expenditures for these critical public roles risk being crowded out by input subsidies (World Bank 2005).

Donors and NGOs Supportive of Subsidies

Donors supportive of subsidies include most UN agencies, NORAD and local and international NGOs such as Oxfam, ActionAid, Plan International etc. They support the programme on the basis that fertiliser is critical to boosting production and assuring food security, and that phasing out subsidies over time, once farmers have ratcheted up their capacity, is the best option. The basic argument of these donors is that agriculture in Malawi cannot survive without subsidies and that subsidies will not distort the market because the private sector is almost non-existent. Besides, without some kind of pan-territorial subsidies, they point out, some areas in the country would not be served at all because of the extremely high costs of doing business in remote areas. According to the FAO office in Malawi, 'it is much cheaper and cost effective to provide an input subsidy than food aid in the face of crisis. At least, the people could plant and produce the food that they require. This is much more dignified than to perpetually receive food handouts' (IRIN 2007:1).

The view of this group of donors is that subsidies can lead to net welfare gains by encouraging an expansion in fertiliser use toward the socially optimal level (IFDC 2003; Pender, Nkonya and Rosegrant 2004). They argue that the current uptake of fertiliser in Malawi is very low (estimated at about 34 kg per hectare against the recommended maximum of 150 kg depending on input-output ratios). This is typical of sub-Saharan Africa, where farmers have generally lagged far behind other developing areas in fertiliser use. The average intensity of fertiliser use throughout sub-Saharan Africa is roughly 8 kg/ha, while in Latin America it is 54 kg/ha. In this narrative, subsidies are seen as an ideal means of kickstarting a process of innovation or scaling up activity that will increase agricultural productivity in the medium to long term, if not in the short term. This view received a major boost from the high-publicity given to the Millennium Village Project (MVP) in Malawi in this period, an initiative that has received much scorn from other donors. The MVP concept is about an integrated package of interventions at the village level thought to be essential to help villages get out of extreme poverty. The package comprises investments in agriculture and environment, health and nutrition, infrastructure, energy and communication and education and training in villages or conglomerations of villages (Cabral, Farrington and Ludi 2006).

The pro-subsidy view also builds on the Sachs-Bono position that subsidies are the only sure way to achieve food security in most of the developing world. The argument is that, once farmers have fertiliser, improved seed and good water management, developing countries like Malawi can achieve food security. Thus, for these countries to achieve a green revolution, farmers have to have access to cheap agricultural inputs at whatever cost. NGOs argue that the need for subsidies is a clear vindication of the failure of the neo-liberal economic reforms that Malawi and other African countries have been implementing since the beginning of the 1980s (Owusu and Ng'ambi 2002; Oxfam 2002; Harrigan 2005). NGOs backed the subsidy programme with the argument that bringing in the social costs of food insecurity and aid dependence shifts the balance in favour of productive subsidy of agriculture. In the final analysis, the NGO vision is for universal fertiliser subsidy but implemented in a phased manner in order to ensure affordability. NGOs further advocate for the institutionalisation of the subsidy programme for purposes of ensuring predictability and facilitating planning among farmers.

Some NGOs subscribe to the lead role of the private sector in spearheading agricultural development but emphasise that government nonetheless has a key role in helping to create markets, where they are missing, through effective and predictable targeted interventions and the introduction of regulations to make markets function properly. They further argue that donors, beyond saving lives in emergencies, should refocus and increase their aid towards preventing crises and promoting livelihoods by supporting subsidies and broader food-security interventions that are known to be cheaper and more cost-effective over time than large-scale emergency responses.

The three main positions and narratives of donors are summed up in Table 5.1.

Impact of the Subsidy Programme

The implementation of the 2005/2006 fertiliser subsidy programme was fairly successful despite a number of glaring shortfalls. For instance, many stakeholders argued that using chiefs and local leaders as custodians of the coupons led to widespread corruption. They also observed that the programme was over-

Table 5.1 : Donor Narratives and Evidence on Fertiliser Subsidies

Donors and their Positions	Narratives	Evidence
Totally opposed to subsidies: • IMF • USAID	• subsidies risk crowding out the private sector • subsidies create market distortions and displace public infrastructure investment • targeting extremely difficult to achieve	• smallholder annual demand for fertiliser estimated at 200,000 against 150,000 target for the subsidy programme • uncertainty over fertiliser prices, as happened during the 2004/2005 growing season
Willing to engage with subsidies: • DFID • World Bank • EU	• capacity challenges for government to properly target subsidies, which are desirable only in exceptional cases of market failure • subsidies fiscally unsustainable if they become part of a long-term development strategy • need for predictability of subsidies in terms of size and duration	• SP/TIP as clear examples of lack of fiscal sustainability (donors withdrew overtime leaving DFID as a sole donor) • high incidence of poverty and vulnerability • problematic targeting (beneficiaries not really making productive use of inputs)
Supportive of subsidies: • Action Aid • NORAD • Oxfam • Plan International • UN agencies such as FAO WFP	• promotion of viable livelihoods rather than perpetual crisis management • agriculture cannot survive without subsidies because of high costs of transport • no market distortions because the private sector does not exist • net welfare gains by promoting optimal use of fertilisers • need for subsidies underscoring failure of neo-liberal reforms	• high levels of poverty exacerbated by the failure of neo-liberal reforms • uptake of fertiliser is currently very limited, estimated at 34 kg/ha against the recommended rate of 150 kg/ha

whelmed by logistical problems with regard to planning and distribution of the farm inputs (Chirwa, Kydd and Doward 2006; IRIN 2007). Chiefs were accused of selling coupons to people who already had money to buy fertiliser. The opposition accused the government of manipulating the coupon system by favouring areas that supported the ruling party. Thus, for the opposition, the fertiliser subsidy was abused to draw people into supporting the DPP. While acknowledging some problems with the coupon system, the government placed the blame on opposition parties. The president conceded that, in some cases, coupons were not given to the intended beneficiaries but said this was because the opposition parties were stealing the fertiliser in order to create a crisis by buying subsidised fertiliser in bulk.

Nevertheless, the impact of the subsidy programme on maize yield was unprecedented. Contrary to the fears of the donors and technical experts, Malawi enjoyed its biggest-ever harvest of 2.6 million metric tonnes of maize, at least half a million tonnes more than its annual requirement of two million metric tonnes. The success of the programme is a subject of continuing debate, however. This debate revolves around whether the huge surplus maize harvest should be attributed to the favourable rains or to the subsidy programme. In the absence of any comprehensive assessment of the programme's impact, the popular view is that the record harvest is a result of the subsidy programme, a perception that has been hyped by the success narratives orchestrated mainly by the government and donors supportive of subsidies. The shift in the positions of those donors who were initially critical of the programme has further strengthened and solidified the success narrative.

Doward et al. (2007) provide a preliminary analysis of the impact of the 2005/2006 fertiliser subsidy programme, using anecdotal evidence in some cases. According to this assessment, incremental fertiliser use on maize as a result of the 2005/2006 subsidy is estimated to be around 45,000 tonnes. This translated into a record harvest of 2.72 million against the backdrop of favourable rainfall patterns. A comparison is drawn to the experience of the 1999/2000 growing season, when Malawi registered a 2.5 million metric tonne harvest with the aid of Starter Pack and good rains. It is projected that the incremental maize production is within the range of 300,000 to 400,000 metric tonnes. The conclusion of Doward et al. is that the 2005/2005 subsidy programme had a positive impact on maize production estimated in the range of 15 to 22 per cent of total production. The programme has also reportedly had a positive impact on the livelihoods of the people. The main reason for this is that the prices of maize generally remained low during the 2006/2007 growing period while *ganyu* (casual labour) rates increased by 50 per cent in kwacha, which with lower maize prices suggests increases in real wage rates of 75 per cent or more (Doward et al. 2007). This is a welcome development because the regressive impact of *ganyu* in creating and perpetuating a vicious circle of poverty and food insecurity is widely recognised in the mainstream contemporary discourse about poverty in the country. In recent years, not only have households that create opportunities for *ganyu* become very limited, but *ganyu* itself has become exceedingly exploitative. The lower maize prices have, therefore, increased the power of *ganyu* labourers to bargain for better wages.

On the other hand, the impact of the subsidy programme on the private-sector fertiliser industry has been particularly felt on sales. It is estimated that the subsidy programme has negatively affected the development of the agro-dealer network that had been taking shape since the advent of liberalization. Most stakeholders pointed out that a good number of dealers have closed out their retail networks. Based on interviews with private-sector stakeholders, and further confirmed by Dorward (2007), it appears that 60 to 70 per cent of the retail outlets closed as a result of reduced retail sales during the 2005/2006 growing season. This should not be surprising because, as observed above, the share of private-sector fertiliser sales tumbled from 87 per cent in the 2004/2005 growing season to 41 per cent during the 2005/2006 season.

The negative impacts of the programme have not been given much attention, however. Consequently, the good rains of the 2005/2006 growing season and the relatively effective management of the fertiliser subsidy programme meant a bumper harvest was produced and the food insecurity of previous years was eliminated. Strikingly, the experiences of the 2005/2006 subsidy programme had, for the first time in many years, challenged the dominant positions of donors in policy-making within the agricultural sector. Thus, the sceptical donors, previously so influential in policy-making in aid-dependent Malawi, were side-stepped. Donors had responded to the state's weak policy-making by increasingly stepping into the government's shoes, substituting for it in the policy function (Sahley et al. 2005; Booth et al. 2005). As a result, agricultural policy processes in Malawi have been subjected to competing views, interests and demands that have compromised policy coherence and subjected policy-making and implementation to ideological leanings. However, in the 2005/2006 growing season, the government, operating within the framework of domestic politics, set a policy agenda for the agricultural sector and determinedly implemented it.

Nevertheless, a conclusive assessment of the impact of the 2005/2006 subsidy programme may be premature. A number of issues remain to be dealt with in order to estimate the positive impact of the subsidy programme with precision. These include, most notably, the fiscal sustainability of the programme, the impact on the private sector and the efficiency of ADMARC as compared to the private sector. Meanwhile, the success narrative, coupled with some indications of positive impacts in highly visible aspects of the programme, are raising the profile of subsidies as a possible magic wand for the problem of food insecurity that had become more or less endemic over the last two decades.

Donor Responses to the Subsidy Programme

How did donors respond to the outcome of the subsidy programme? Following much debate, a certain reluctant pragmatism emerged. The change in the positions of donor agencies vis-à-vis their earlier uncompromising stance on the fertiliser subsidy challenges the narratives espoused at their headquarters. This is particularly underscored by their willingness to undertake a series of studies on the subsidy programme with a view to informing their future engagement with the government. The agencies demonstrated a readiness to rise above their often ideologically-driven policy narratives for a meaningful trade-off with the prevailing realities in the Malawian context. The World Bank, for example, is strongly wedded to a liberalisation narrative. It emphasises that the revitalisation of African agriculture is critically dependent on the implementation of unfinished market reforms in order to promote and entrench the leading role of the private sector and NGOs in agricultural development (Cabral and Scoones 2006). As for DFID, while subscribing to the broad regulatory role of the state, it entrusts the state with the task of kickstarting rural markets, especially in poorly resourced, remote rural areas where high transaction costs and coordination failures constrain private-sector development. Targeted subsidies are supported as temporary measures to remove barriers for private-sector participation in markets (Cabral and Scoones 2006).

The donors' change from their initial positions was inevitable when it became evident that the Malawian government was unwilling and politically unable to be compliant and accept their demands. This is explained by the fact that state legitimacy in Malawi is closely linked to the availability of maize or, more broadly, food security. The divisions among donors, fostered by competing ideological orientations, had to be patched up. Business had to carry on, especially since, due in part to fortuitous weather conditions, the programme was remarkably successful. Given the government's determination to implement the subsidy programme, the donors had to accept that there was no alternative to backing the government's political decision. The donors' behaviour was political too. Their turnaround smacks of political opportunism, especially in view of the fact that the turnaround was justified as an attempt to be in tune with the government's own priorities and commitments.

It is not surprising, therefore, that, during 2006, a reconfiguring of actors took place around a new, more coherent policy narrative. A group of donors including DFID, USAID and the World Bank commissioned studies to learn from the lessons of the 2005/2006 experience, which seemed to encourage a backing away of the downright anti-subsidy line. In its place, a set of conditions for donor support for the subsidy programme were suggested. These included the following:

- greater involvement of the private sector in both the procurement and the distribution of subsidised fertiliser and other farm inputs on equal terms with ADMARC and SFFRFM;

- promotion of choice among beneficiaries in terms of the range of fertilisers involved and the outlets for fertilisers and seeds;

- extension of the subsidy intervention to other crops besides maize and tobacco in order to promote crop diversification;

- development of plans for marketing and storage, especially during times of excess production.

The realities of the domestic political economy and policy-process context of Malawi had forced the policy process to move on. Populist maize politics had won out over sound economic policies, at least from the perspective of the donors. An alternative viewpoint was that democracy had succeeded in the face of interfering pressure from donors, For others, a sensible pragmatism had arisen through negotiation, reviewing evidence and overcoming ideological positions.

The experiences of the 2005/2006 fertiliser subsidy programme regarding the trade-offs between various stakeholders, including the evolution of donors' reactions, clearly underscore the fact that policy-making is a political process. It is not simply the instrumental execution of rational decisions (Keeley and Scoones 2003). It is evident from the events leading to the implementation of the programme that policies should be conceptualised as courses of action, elements of ongoing processes of negotiation and bargaining between multiple actors over time. This involves focusing on the intersections and negotiations of knowledge, power and politics.

The Emergence of a Developmental State in Malawi?

The successful implementation of the 2005/2006 fertiliser subsidy programme, culminating in a dramatic decline in the severity of the food-security problem in the country for the first time in nearly 20 years, is a significant achievement. There is no doubt that the subsidy programme greatly enhanced the stature and legitimacy of the state machinery. The ability of the government to put food on the table enhanced its credibility in the eyes of the people. Thus, the people are now able to identify themselves with the state by pointing not only to a tangible state service but also a service that has a direct bearing on their very basis of existence.

But does this portend the re-emergence of a developmental state in Malawi? Privileged with the benefit of hindsight, it could be argued that Banda's one-party state displayed some attributes of a developmental state compared to the experiences after the transition to democracy in May 1994. There were systematic efforts, mediated through development policies, to achieve economic growth and development. The regime had a clearly articulated vision of what it wanted to achieve, including how to go about achieving its goals. The huge dent, however, in the one-party state's development endeavours was the blatant exploitation of the masses due to both the development strategies themselves and the failure to distribute the benefits of development fairly. Instead of trickle-down, there was trickle-up; the benefits of development went only to a minority of the population. In other words, the state was captured by a small ruling class commandeered by what Mhone (1992) characterised as the triumvirate. For this reason, the history of the one-party state has been generally characterised as one of monumental democratic and development failure. In effect, the one-party state was an autocratic developmental state serving only the interests of a few at the expense of the masses.

The transition to democracy potentially signalled an opportunity to reconstitute a developmental state with the ability to clearly articulate its development goals but substantially democratic in nature. The transition provided the opportunity to propagate and institutionalise a viable developmental state, a state that not only embodies the principles of electoral democracy but also ensures citizens' participation in development and governance processes (Edigheji 2005). However, as demonstrated in this paper, the capacity of the state in policy-making and implementation has deteriorated tremendously since May 1994 even though there are some incipient signs of recovery. Technical capacity was decimated, patronage and corruption proliferated and there was complete lack of policy direction, as evidenced by the multiplicity of, and the enormous overlaps in, the various policy documents and initiatives. The major consequence of government's dismal incapacity in policy processes was that donors effectively replaced it as the state's policy maker.

It is not surprising, therefore, that the success of the 2005/2006 fertiliser subsidy programme is widely celebrated as a notable success story and, in some circles, projected as a possible blueprint for future policy-making processes in the country. The optimistic view is that the experiences with 2005/2006 fertiliser subsidy programme can serve as a useful starting point for resurrecting the developmental state in Malawi. Moreover, a democratic framework, considered key to the establishment of a viable developmental state in contemporary development discourse, is in place, even though it is still fragile in certain respects.

The major positive lesson from the 2005/2006 fertiliser subsidy programme is that the government has been able to reclaim its rightful role of setting the development agenda based on the priorities of its citizenry. The implementation of the subsidy programme was almost revolutionary, given the history of donor dominance in the country's policy-making processes, especially within the agricultural sector. It is striking to note that the government did not recoil even in the face of fierce donor resistance to the programme but proceeded without the support of the donor community. The fact that donors later reconsidered their initial hard-line positions and became willing to engage with the programme is an instructive development. It has given government the confidence that it can meaningfully engage with donors in a bid to assert priorities that are responsive to the needs of its constituents. In fact, one of the key attributes of a developmental state is that it should be able to clearly set out its development objectives. Thus, the state must be in a position to behave as a coherent actor able to identify and implement development goals (Edigheji 2005; Bull 2006; Mbabazi and Taylor 2005). The ability of the government to negotiate with donors is quite critical in hedging against the 'depoliticized quest for technocratic governance now pushed by international financial institutions (IFIs) in which technocracy is supposed to carry out policies that are good for the nation for no apparent reason, not even self-serving ones' (Mkandawire 1998:3).

The main challenge to building on this positive aspect of the fertiliser subsidy programme in the quest to establish a developmental state relates to the politics that led to its adoption and implementation. Leftwich (1995) places a considerable premium on the role of politics as one of the critical determinants of the nature and shape of a developmental state. It is very clear that the fertiliser subsidy politics in Malawi were very different from the idealised politics described by Leftwich. The politics that led to the adoption and implementation of the subsidy programme were not driven by a collective common good but rather by the myopic political interests of the various stakeholders in the political arena. It could as well be argued that it was quite accidental that these politics facilitated the adoption and implementation of the subsidy programme. The subsidy proposals united the government (understood as comprising both the ruling party and the opposition) as a collective actor because food security lies at the core of the legitimacy of governance. It is a huge political risk for any stakeholder to oppose initiatives of this nature; doing so would be shooting oneself in the foot. Whether one is in government or not, food security is a key issue that has to be given priority. Thus, no faction was against support for the agricultural sector; the debate was about the strategies of how to provide support so as to ensure that all constituencies were served. It is doubtful, therefore, whether the fertiliser subsidy politics could be successfully transferred to any other policy process.

The problem of technical capacity in the policy-making function is yet to be addressed. In a critical review of social-protection policy, Chinsinga (2007c) observes that the government machinery is yet to recover from huge deficiencies in the skills, expertise and experience that are key to handling policy processes. As a result, donor dominance still prevails. Thus, there is an urgent need to invest in strengthening the capacity of the government agencies entrusted with policy functions in terms of both people and systems in planning, coordination and implementation. This is a key concern because the institutional or organisational capacity of the state, including its relations to surrounding social structures, is vital to the success of a developmental state. In particular, a powerful, competent and insulated bureaucracy is considered as an extremely important feature of the developmental state (Leftwich 1995; Mkandawire 1998; Mbabazi and Taylor 2005). There is no doubt that the experiences with the 2005/2006 fertiliser subsidy could be a precursor for resurrecting the developmental state in Malawi, but it is perhaps too early to fully project it as such. The potential of these experiences could easily be overestimated, especially given the unique nature of the politics of food security in the country. Nevertheless, these experiences provide considerable food for thought.

Notes

1. The African state was variously described as the rentier state, the overextended state, the parasitical state, the patrimonial state, the prebendal state, the crony state, the kleptocratic state and the inverted state. For details, see Mkandawire 1998.

2. Doubts have, however, been expressed as to whether Mutharika's politics of policy-making shall be significantly different predecessor regimes. The argument is that he might have a genuine desire to transform the way government works but his efforts are more likely to be undermined by the stark realities of Malawi's politics. This is the case patronage is deeply entrenched and embedded as an organizing framework for politics in the country and any kind of radical reforms will have contend with its enduring logic (cf. Sahely, et al., 2005 and Booth, et al., 2006).

References

Amsden, A., 1989, *Asia's Next Giant: South Korea and Late Industrialization*, New York: Oxford University Press

Archaya, S., 1978, 'Perspectives and Problems of Development in Low Income Sub-Saharan Africa', *World Bank Staff Working Paper No. 300*, Washington DC: World Bank

Bird, K., Booth, D. and Pratt, N., 2003, *The Contribution of Politics, Policy Failures, and Bad Governance to the Food Security Crisis in Southern Africa*, Forum for Food Security in Southern Africa. (www.odi.or.uk/food-security-forum). 15 August 2008.

Booth, D., Cammack, D., Harrigan, J., Kanyongolo, E., Mataure, M. and Ngwira, N., 2006, 'Drivers of Change and Development in Malawi', *Working Paper No. 261*, London: Overseas Development Institute.

Bull, B., 2006, 'The Development Theory Revisited', in Banik, D., ed., *Poverty, Politics and Development: Interdisciplinary Perspectives*, Bergen: Fagbokforlaget.

Cabral, L. and Scoones, I., 2006, *What Role for Ministries of Agriculture? Narratives and Policy Space*, Paper presented at the Future Agricultures Workshop, Brighton, UK, 21-22 March.

Cabral, L., Farrington, J., and Ludi, E., 2006, 'The Millennium Village Project: A New Approach to Ending Rural Poverty in Africa?' *Natural Resource Perspectives* Vol. 101.

Cammack, P., 2002, 'Neoliberalism, the World Bank and the New Politics of Development', in U. Kothari and M. Minogue, M., eds., *Development Theory and Practice: Critical Perspectives*, Basingstoke: Palgrave.

Chikulo, B., 1998, 'Decentralization and the Role of the State in Future', in I. Mandaza, ed., *Governance and Human Development in Southern Africa: Selected Essays*, Harare: SAPES.

Chimphonda, S., and Dzoole-Mwale, V., 2005, *The Status of the Agricultural Sector in Malawi: A Parliamentarian's Perspective*, Lilongwe: Parliamentary Committee on Agriculture and Natural Resources.

Chinsinga, B., 2002, 'The Politics of Poverty Alleviation in Malawi: A Critical Review', in E. Englund, ed., *A Democracy of Chameleons: Politics and Culture in the New Malawi*, Stockholm: Nordiska Afrikainstitutet, Elanders Golab.

Chinsinga, B., 2003a, 'The Participatory Development Approach under a Microscope: The Case of the Poverty Alleviation Programme in Malawi', *Journal of Social Development in Africa*, Vol. 18, No. 2, pp. 129-144.

Chinsinga, B., 2003b, 'Can Developing Nations be Strategic Actors in the Global Village?', *Journal Of Cultural Studies*, Vol, 5, No. 2, pp. 151-181.

Chinsinga, B., 2003c, 'Lack of Alternative Leadership in Democratic Malawi: Some Reflections ahead of the 2004 General Elections', *Journal of Nordic African Studies*, Vol. 12, No. 1, pp. 1-22.

Chinsinga, B., 2004, 'Poverty and Food Security in Malawi: Some Policy Reflections on the Context of Crumbling Traditional Support Systems', *Canadian Journal of Development Studies*, Vol. 25, No. 2, pp. 321-341.

Chinsinga, B., 2007a, 'Reclaiming Policy Space: Lessons from Malawi's Fertilizer Subsidy Programme', Paper Presented at the World Development Workshop, IDS, University of Sussex 21-24 January.

Chinsinga, B., 2007b, 'Public Policymaking' in N. Patel and L. Svasand, eds., *Government and Politics in Malawi*, Balaka: Montfort Media.

Chinsinga, B., 2007c, *Social Protection Policy in Malawi: Processes, Politics and Challenges*, Draft for Future Agricultures Consortium (FAC), Institute of Development Studies, University of Sussex.

Chinsinga, B., Dulani, B., and Kayuni, H., 2003, *2003 Winter Targeted Input Programme (TIP) Evaluation Study*, Study Commissioned for the Ministry of Agriculture, Irrigation and Food Security by the UK Department for International Development, Lilongwe: Ministry of Agriculture, Irrigation and Food Security.

Chipeta, C., 1993, 'The Impact of Structural Adjustment on the People of Malawi', *The Impact of Structural Adjustment on the Population of Africa*, London: James Currey.

Chirwa, E., 1995, 'Impact of Food Security and Nutrition Intervention Projects in Malawi', Draft report submitted to the Food Security and Nutrition Unit, National Economic Council, Lilongwe, Malawi.

Chirwa, E., 1997, 'Fostering Private Food Marketing and Food Supplies after Liberalization in Sub-Saharan Africa: The Case of Malawi', Draft report submitted to WIDER, the United Nations University.

Chirwa, E., Kydd, J. and Doward, A., 2006, 'Future Scenarios for Agriculture in Malawi: Challenges and Dilemmas', Paper presented at the Future Agricultures Consortium held at the Institute of Development Studies, University of Sussex, 20-21 March.

Clark, J., 1991, *Democratizing Development: The Role of Voluntary Organizations*, London: Earthscans.

Devereux, S., Baulch, B., Phiri, A. and Sabates-Wheeler, R., 2006, *Vulnerability to Chronic Poverty and Malnutrition in Malawi*, Lilongwe: DFID Malawi.

Donovan, G., 2004, *Fertilizer Subsidies in sub-Saharan Africa: A Policy Note* (Draft), Washington, DC: World Bank.

Dorward, A., 2007, *Evaluation of the 2006/2007 Agricultural Input Supply Programme, Malawi:* London: Imperial College, Wadonda Consult, Michigan State University and Overseas Development Institute.

Dulani, B., 2005, 'Consolidating Malawi's Democracy? An Analysis of the 2004 Malawi General Elections', *Africa Insight*, Vol. 36, pp. 3-12.

Edigheji, O., 2005, 'A Democratic Developmental State in Africa? A Concept Paper', *Research Report 105*, Johannesburg: Centre for Policy Studies.

Fozzard, A. and Simwaka, C., 2002, 'How, When and Why does Poverty get Priority? Poverty Reduction Strategy and Public Expenditure in Malawi', *Working Paper No. 166*, London: Overseas Development Institute.

Government of Malawi/World Bank, 2006, *Malawi Poverty and Vulnerability Assessment: Investing in Our Future*, Lilongwe: Government Printer.

Harrigan, J., 2001, *From Dictatorship to Democracy: Economic Policy in Malawi 1964-2000*, London: Ashgate.

Harrigan, J., 2005, 'U-Turns and Full Circles: Two Decades of Agricultural Reform in Malawi 1981-2000', *World Development*, Vol. 31, No. 5, pp. 847-862.

IFDC, 2003, 'Input Subsidies and Agricultural Development: Issues and Options for Developing and Transitional Economies', *Discussion Paper Series 29*, Muscle Shoals, AL: International Fertilizer Development Centre.

IRIN, 2007, *Glitches in Key Agriculture Subsidy Programme*, Nairobi: Integrated Regional Information Network. (www://allafrica.com/stories/printable/20070190426.html). 1 September 2007.

Jenkins, R. and Tsoka, M., 'Malawi', *Fighting Poverty in Africa: Are PRSPS Making a Difference?* London: Overseas Development Institute.

Kaluwa, B., Ngalande, E., Chilowa, W. and Silumbu, E., 1992, *The Structural Adjustment Programmes in Malawi: A Case of Successful Adjustment?* Harare SAPES.

Keeley, J. and Scoones, I., 2003, *Understanding Environmental Policy Processes: Cases from Africa*, London: Earthscan.

Kishindo, P., 1997, 'Malawi's Social Development Policies: A Historical Review', *Bwalo*, Issue No. 1, pp. 11-20.

Leftwich, A., 1995, 'Bringing Politics Back In: Towards a Model of the Developmental State', *Journal of Development Studies*, Vol. 31, No. 3.

Levy, S., 2005, *Starter Packs: A Strategy to Fight Hunger in Developing Countries? Lessons from the Malawi Experience 1998-2003*, Oxford: CABI Publishing.

Mbabazi, P. and Taylor, I., 2005, 'Botswana and Uganda as Developmental States?' in P. Mbabazi and I. Taylor, eds., *The Potentiality of Developmental States in Africa: Botswana and Uganda Compared*, Dakar: CODESRIA.

Mhone, G., 1987, 'Agriculture and Food Security in Malawi: A Review', in T. Mkandawire, ed., *The State and Agriculture in Africa*, Dakar: CODESRIA.

Mhone, G., 1992, 'The Political Economy of Malawi: An Overview', in G. Mhone, ed., *Malawi at the Crossroads: The Postcolonial Political Economy*, Harare: SAPES.

Mkandawire, T., 1998, *Thinking about Developmental States in Africa*. (www.unu.edu/hq/academic/Pg_area4/Mkandawire.html). 15 August 2008.

Mvula, P., Chirwa, E. and Kadzandira, J., 2003, 'Poverty and Social Impact Assessment in Malawi: Closure of ADMARC Markets', Draft final report submitted to Social Development Department, World Bank and Economic Section/PRSP Support, GTZ.

Nakhumwa, T., 2005, *Rapid Evaluation of the 2005 Fertilizer Subsidy Programme in Malawi*, Lilongwe: Civil Society Agriculture Network and Malawi Economic Justice Network.

Nation, 2004, 'Fertilizer Price to Go Down, Says PS for Agriculture', Lilongwe: The Nation, 25 June.

Nation, 2005, 'ADMARC Only Buying Maize', Lilongwe: The Nation, 17 August.

Ngwira, N., 2002, 'Participatory National Planning: Lessons of Experience from Malawi's Vision 2020', in D. Milanzi, M. Mulinge and E. Mukaamabo, eds., *Democracy, Human Rights and Regional Cooperation in Southern Africa*, Pretoria: Africa Institute of South Africa.

Nzunda, M. and Ross, M., 1995, *Church, Law and Political Transition in Malawi 1992-1994*, Gweru: Mambo Press.

Owusu, K. and Ng'ambi, E., 2002, *Structural Damage: The Causes and Consequences of the Malawi Food Crisis*. (www.wdm.org.org.ukImplications). 15 August 2008.

Oxfam, 2002, 'Death on the Doorstep of the Summit', Oxfam Briefing Paper, Oxford: Oxfam.

Pender, J., Nkonya, E., Rosegrant, M., 2004, 'Soil Fertility and Fertilizer Subsidies in sub-Saharan Africa: Issues and Recommendations', PowerPoint presentation Washington DC: IFPRI.

Pryor, F., 1990, *The Political Economy of Poverty, Equity and Growth: Malawi and Madagascar*, Oxford: Oxford University Press.

Sahley, C., Groelsema, B., Marchione, T. and Nelson, D., 2005, *The Governance Dimensions of Food Security in Malawi*, Lilongwe: USAID.

Simon, D., 2002, 'Neoliberalism, Structural Adjustment and Poverty Reduction Strategies', in V. Desai and R. Potter, eds, *The Companion to Development Studies*, New York: Oxford University Press.

Stambuli, K., 2002, *Long-run Food Security of a Top-down Agricultural Strategy in Malawi*, Surrey: Surrey Institute for Global Economic Research.

UNDP, 1996, *Human Development Report*, New York: Oxford University Press.

Van Donge, J., Chirvala, M., Kapondamgaga, P., Kapasila, W., Mgemezulu, O., Sangore, N. and Thawani, E., 2002, 2000-2001 Targeted Input Programme Module 2: A Qualitative Study of Markets and Livelihood Security in Malawi: Lilongwe

World Bank, 1982, *Malawi National Rural Programme (NRDP) Review*, Washington DC: World Bank.

World Bank, 1989, *Sub-Saharan Africa: From Crisis to Sustainable Growth*, Washington DC: World Bank.

World Bank, 2005, *Agricultural Growth for the Poor: An Agenda for Development*, Washington DC: World Bank.